ASSESSING LEARNING

A CAEL Handbook for Faculty

Susan Simosko and Associates

Council for Adult and Experiential Learning
10840 Little Patuxent Parkway, Suite #203
Columbia, Maryland 21044

For Jack Arbolino and Walter Shea

Table of Contents

Prologue

In preparing this book, we have made several assumptions:

- that people can and do learn throughout their entire lives in a variety of ways;

- that much of what people learn is comparable to the content of the curriculum that is offered in colleges and universities throughout the country;

- that there are valid and reliable means of assessing peoples' extracollegiate learning in light of college and university and curriculum;

- that in recognizing the college-level learning acquired by adults outside the formal college classroom, we are fostering the growth and self confidence of individuals and the academic flexibility and efficiency of our educational institutions; and

- that, in the end, the real benefit to be gained by more flexible and responsive educational providers is a society better able to accommodate itself to the pressures and demands of an increasingly complex world.

It is in this context that this book was prepared. It is intended to give the reader a glimpse into the basic tenets and assumptions that make the assessment of prior learning work; to offer a set of effective guidelines for setting standards; to provide a review of some of the proven techniques and practices that have been used to evaluate the learning; to address a series of issues relevant to particular subject matter areas; and to give examples of working institutional models and new initiatives in the recognition of prior learning.

Writers on this topic would be remiss, of course, if they assumed that the process of assessing adults' learning is simply a matter of techniques, procedures and institutional models. For anyone who has been even remotely engaged in the process of evaluating learning, it is obvious that this is not the case. The assessment xii

or evaluation of learning has always been, since some of the earliest considerations of Western thinking, central to the understanding of the human endeavor. For centuries epistemological inquiry has asked, "What is knowledge?" Philosophers and laymen alike have looked at the "evidence" for their various hypotheses; they have offered their ideas and set their theories down on paper.

It is our contention that the work and issues described in this book are responding to the same basic question, "What is knowledge?" Extending that question we find ourselves asking other, related questions: What is learning? What is achieved in the learning process? How do we know, really know, what any of our students, whether 19 or 45, know and what they can do? Do we know what even we, ourselves, know and can do? How do we know what makes an educated person? What does having a college education mean? What relationship, if any, is there between an educated person and an effective worker or citizen? To our way of thinking, these are the highly relevant questions that place the assessment of peoples' learning at the heart of the educational process at any level and in almost every context. While we have attempted to make this book a helpful handbook in the assessment of adults' learning, it is in the spirit of this intellectual inquiry that the assessment of prior learning needs to be considered if it is to continue to flourish as an integral part of an educational system designed to foster a diverse, creative, and educated populace.

As teachers, most of us spend our working lives imparting knowledge. Some, to be sure, are also concerned with the process of learning and with students' ability to communicate in one way or another what has been taught. But by and large, as instructors or teachers, we impart knowledge, information, technical expertise; we focus our attention on providing input. Rare is the teacher who sees him or herself as the facilitator of a student's active learning and the evaluator or assessor of that student's progression in a lifelong process of learning. Although each year thousands, if not millions, of grades are dispensed and placed meaningfully on transcripts, few of us consciously consider our roles as evaluators. Yet as evaluators or assessors we need to focus on the **outcomes** of learning—those skills and fields of knowledge individuals come to master, whether with our assistance or without. The adult students coming to us are rich in learning; they come to us seeking an evaluation or verification of their competence. Unlike our role as traditional teacher, our role of assessor does not give us the opportunity to supply our inputs.

Adult students offer us evidence of their learning—products, performances, external documentation. These are the **outcomes** of their learning. As faculty members engaged in the process of assessing these students, it is our job to evaluate, make judgments about these outcomes of learning. To do so we need to know what we expect of students at various levels in our disciplines and develop fair and reliable methods of assuring the evaluation of a particular student's achievement in light of those expectations. It is to this purpose, that this book is dedicated.

As we begin to look at the outcomes of learning, rather than only the inputs, we have the opportunity to acknowledge the strength and importance of individualized diverse learning and achievement. We hope that this volume will help the reader gain a perspective on his or her professional work that will enhance the educational process for all. And actually, of course, who among us is not at heart both teacher and learner?

Acknowledgment

This volume is quite obviously a group effort. The contributors all gave freely of their time and effort. To each I want to extend a personal thank you not only for a job well done but also for the dedication and commitment to the idea of this volume and the work it represents.

A thank you is also extended to each of the institutions represented. By their example and innovation, they have enabled thousands of adult students to move in new directions, educationally and professionally. We hope that other institutions will follow the example of these pioneering institutions.

I want also to extend a special thank you to Morris Keeton and Mary Ellis for their continued support and constructive criticism throughout the process of the book's development. Certainly without the vision and involvement of the thousands of committed professionals in the CAEL network, a volume of this sort would not be possible.

A special thank you is also extended to Robin Halnon and Mike Morucci for their patience and good humor in typing all these many pages more than once.

I want also to thank the W.K. Kellogg Foundation, which, through its commitment to establishing a national network of adult learner services, contributed significantly to the preparation of this book.

To Graham Debling I extend a very special thank you for two-years' worth of conversation and insight on issues in assessment and for his constructive comments and support in putting the finishing touches on this book.

Lastly, I want to thank all those college faculty and adult students who in workshops, letters, telephone conversations and sometimes through seemingly telepathic means have helped to ask the probing questions that have led us to search for answers and share what we think we have learned.

Susan Simosko
January, 1988

Introduction

Susan Simosko

It is Friday afternoon. You are sitting at your desk waiting for a prospective new student to show up. The information supplied to you by the Admissions Office tells you that she is 39, employed at a local bank, the mother of three children and that she's considering majoring in psychology, your field of expertise.

As you sit there, looking at the huge stack of papers to be graded over the weekend, you wonder about the university's new policy to attract adult students. The facts and figures tell you that traditional enrollments are down for the third year in a row and that some departments will be scaled back considerably to reflect that trend. You are weary from all the debates in the Faculty Senate about how best to admit adults: should they be required to take the standard admission tests or not? And if not, how will you know they can do college-level work? And what about all this business of college-level learning being acquired off campus, out of the university environment? You are skeptical at best, although you do remember that there was a student a couple of years ago who was able to pass not only the Psych 101 challenge exam you developed but one in Abnormal Behavior as well because of his work and independent reading. But he was an exception.

The knock at the door interrupts your reverie. You want this to be over fast.

Into your office comes Mrs. Barbara Tilton, a tall attractive woman carrying a large brief case. You ask her to sit down and introduce yourself. Then you begin to ask her questions so you can help her determine what her educational choices will be. This is what you learn:

She is assistant treasurer at the bank but has an independent editorial firm with her husband. One of her daughters is learning disabled and from that circumstance stems her interest in psychology. She has been writing for and editing a regional newsletter for a parents' group concerned about learning disabled children, and last

year she was invited to speak to a State-government task force looking into the educational needs of learning disabled students. She
tells you this story in a rush, her energy a pleasant contrast to that
of the vast majority of 18 and 19 year old students who often sit
slumped and indecisive in the same chair.

She tells you all in one breath that she wants to leave the banking profession, get her degree, go on to graduate school and become
a psychologist so that people will listen to her and so she will have
more of an opportunity to help others. While earning money is
fine—and necessary—she needs to do something more with her life
than sign cashier checks and let other people make decisions about
her daughter that she often questions. She adds that her husband,
after more than a little convincing, has agreed to support her career
change although they both are aware of the added strain, emotional
and financial, that will be placed on the family once she leaves her
job and begins school. "But finally," she tells you, "we have worked
it out and I need to begin. That's why I'm here. What do I have to do
next?"

You breathe a sigh of relief. This is going to be quick after all.
You pull out the Fact Sheet about the degree programs the University
offers and a second sheet that outlines the various possibilities for
majoring in psychology. You assume that she will take them home,
as you have suggested, make her decisions and that sooner or later
you will see her in class.

Instead though, she sits there reading over what you have given
to her. When she glances up, she is obviously distressed. "You mean
I have to begin as a freshman?" she asks somewhat indignantly. "Er,
yes, that's the way it usually works," you reply with a smile. She
puts the papers on your desk and stares directly into your eyes.
"Look," she says, "I don't have four years. Didn't I make that clear?
I need to get this degree out of the way and get on to graduate
school. I have a family to provide for, a husband whom I want to see
occasionally, and I have a need to get into a new profession. And
aside from all of that, as I look over the courses you are expecting me
to take, I'll bet I already know more than half of your curriculum. So
what am I supposed to do? Waste at least two years of my life sitting
in your classrooms, paying money for information and skills I
already possess?"

There is an awkward silence. "Well," you begin, rather limply,
"I'm sure we could design some challenge exams for you . . . "
"Challenge exams?" she exclaims, digging into her brief case. "I

thought this university was interested in attracting and helping adults earn their degrees. That article in the newspaper is the only reason I'm here." With that, she begins to put all sorts of papers and books on your desk. "See this?" she says, "I wrote it. And this one and this one and this one. And see these? These I edited. And here are examples of the work I do at the bank. And here is a list of the books I've read in the past couple of years. And here are the syllabi of training programs I've attended sponsored by the American Banking Institute. And all you can talk about are a few challenge exams. Really, I thought this was going to be an opportunity for me to focus on psychology. I didn't realize that you'd expect me to take English 101. . . . " Her voice trails off.

You certainly hadn't expected that sort of outburst. But even glancing at the articles and documents she has pushed in front of you, you can tell that if in fact Mrs. Tilton had done the work herself, she probably should be exempt from some of the introductory level courses. Just as you are about to speak, Mrs. Tilton begins again. "I'm sorry for the outburst," she says, "I really am. You just don't know what I've gone through to get to this point—with myself, my husband and my current employer. I was so excited coming over here to think that at last I could begin to act on my decision; I just assumed that it would be easier and take less time. I guess I was wrong, wasn't I?"

"No," you reply, "You weren't wrong to make those assumptions. This University is in the midst of a major transition. We have spent the last 75 years teaching people 18 to 22 years of age what we think is important. Sometimes I'm not sure we even know anymore what's really important. And most recently, the administration has told us that we need to recruit adults, award them credit for learning they obtain from their lives, but frankly, Mrs. Tilton, the only way I've ever done that is by making up a test. But certainly I can see, just by these few things you've shown me that a test in some areas would be absurd for you. What I would like to do is schedule another appointment with you, one in which we will have more time to go over what it is you think you know. I'd like you to take this College catalog with you, along with the other documents I've given you to help you consider not only what it is you think you already know but what you think this University has to offer you in the way of new learning. In the meantime, I will meet with the Dean and several of the department chairs to see if we can develop ways of evaluating your learning for credit and work out a flexible degree plan for you."

Sound familiar? All over the United States and in other parts of the world variations of that conversation are transpiring. Not always with the eventual optimistic tone of the one just presented but, more often than not, with the same urgency. People of all ages, colors, religions, and creeds are desperate for what we have to offer: a chance to improve, change, or enlarge their lives. Whether auto mechanic, airline pilot, dancer, dairy farmer, computer salesperson, dental assistant, or civic volunteer, adult men and women are knocking at the doors of our educational institutions hoping that one more course, a certificate, a degree will enable them to make the life transitions they seek. For some, that transition will mean a new job; for others it will be a chance at a promotion; for still others it means the difference between no job and a first one. For almost all, it will mean a sense of accomplishment, a new sense of self esteem, and an opportunity to grow, intellectually as well as emotionally.

It may come as a surprise to learn that during the past twenty years, students over the age of 25 have become the fastest growing group of the entire college population. Today more than one out of every three college students is over 25 years of age. Yet most of today's colleges are still focusing on meeting the educational needs of the more traditionally-aged student. Is it any wonder that adult students feel frustrated and angry when, for example, advisors have no evening appointments, the registrar's office is only open until 4:30, and required courses are available only during the day-time curriculum?

But the picture is changing. Increasingly colleges and universities are changing. For example, a 1984 survey conducted by the Council for Adult and Experiential Learning (CAEL) of all colleges and universities in the United States revealed that more than 1200 had at least some means of recognizing the learning that adults acquire away from the college campus. Increasingly it would appear that colleges are developing policies by which learning can be recognized for credit by using standardized credit by examination programs or institutionally designed challenge exams. In addition, they are increasingly developing prior learning assessment programs and committing time and money to have faculty properly trained to insure the credibilty of these programs.

The impetus for this new wave of interest in attracting and serving adults has not, of course, come just out of the blue. There are many factors that are contributing to the growth of this trend. One comes from the colleges themselves: the declining enrollment pool of traditionally-aged students has forced some colleges to open their doors to adults. And adults themselves have become wise consumers. It is they who are no longer willing to pay to repeat learning they have already acquired. They have read about the opportunities for credit that are out there and as educated consumers are looking for the program that will best serve their needs. There is also a new urgency to their need for education. As the world economy tightens and job changes become increasingly common, there is a dire need to upgrade skills, acquire new ones, or obtain additional credentials to keep ahead of the next person. And of course, adults are the taxpayers, the employers, the benefactors. Colleges can no longer (if in fact they ever could) go it alone. In many cases they need the support of their local communities to stay in business and often look to a prospering company or union in hopes of support.

Business and industry are providing yet another pressure on colleges and universities. There is the interesting story of a college president who received a phone call from the CEO of a local Fortune 500 company. The CEO was calling to ask why after his company had paid more than $2000 to train a particular employee in a branch of hi-tech data processing, he was now being asked by the college to pay again in the form of tuition reimbursement for that same employee to take the **identical** course taught by the **identical** faculty member who for the last several years had worked for the company as a free lance trainer!

One could cite literally dozens of other examples of why colleges and universities are moving to develop quality programs by which they can evaluate adults' prior learning. Government agencies, the military, volunteer associations, unions, community-action groups all are seeing that education is one of the few "win-win" situations available to people, regardless of background or age. Education—as a process by which people improve their thinking, develop new skills, learn more about the world around them, and see themselves as determiners of their own futures—can only benefit all of us.

In this book we have tried to provide the basic tools by which college faculty and administrators can develop skills and procedures for assessing adults' prior learing. We have raised issues that invariably arise when faculty are first exposed to the notion of assessing such extra-institutional learning and have attempted to offer solutions to some of the more common problems individuals and institutions seem to encounter when they first get started in this work. Most of what is presented comes directly from our practical, hands-on experience of training and working with college faculty and administrators. As an inducement for further learning, bibliographies have been provided. It is our sincere hope that the reader will find this book not only a practical guide but also an enjoyable, helpful book, relevant and applicable to his or her professional growth.

Susan Simosko, author of Earn College Credit for What You Know, has served CAEL both as a member of the central staff and as a consultant. She recently formed her own business in Sheffield, England and provides training, assessment and evaluative services to organizations in Great Britian, the United States and elsewhere. Her address is 20 Chorley Drive, Sheffield, England Sl0 3RR.

Chapter 1
Experiential Learning and Assessment

Susan Simosko

Defining Experiential Learning

No doubt if you have been in the field of education for even just a few years, you have heard terms like "credit for life experience," "experiential learning," "portfolio assessment," or "prior learning assessment." For many people these phrases are similar, if not synonymous, and in many circles have a collective bad name, connoting cheap education and worthless college credit. Often seen as an outgrowth of the turbulence of the Sixties, many faculty can still recall the glaring headline of a 1977 "Change Magazine" article entitled "CLEP and The Great Credit Giveaway" (Stecher, 1977), in which the author, Carl Stecher, claimed that a student need know almost nothing to earn credit based on the recommendations of the American Council on Education for the College Level Examination Program's General Examinations.

The belief of most professional educators at that time and certainly in the decade following is that life experience in and of itself is not worth college credit. And indeed, there is not a professional whose name appears in this book who would not agree with that belief. **College credit should never be awarded for life experience.** NEVER. You will not find "credit for experience" countenanced in this book and if you are about to embark on setting up a program of recognizing peoples' prior learning, you should avoid use of the phrase "credit for experience." It is a red herring and serves only to confuse the issues and undermine the very best of intentions. What we are concerned with in this book is **learning**: the skills, knowledge, and competences that people acquire from their work experience, their volunteer activities, their avocations, their homemaking experience, and their independent reading.

That is why the term "experiential learning" is so important. It serves to describe legitimately most of the learning that occurs in our lives. As babies learning about their environment or young children acquiring new motor skills, we all learn by doing, by trying, by imitating, by experiencing. So too through adolescence and on into adulthood we regularly and routinely learn by experience. From learning to drive a car, to sorting out our interpersonal relationships, to becoming proficient gardeners, cooks, poets, athletes, or teachers, we are all experiential learners and if, for the sake of this book, we are over the age of 22, we are adult learners, too.

We, just like the students who come to our classrooms, have a natural curiosity that leads us to experience something new. That experience often leads to learning and the learning to understanding. From understanding comes the ability to generalize and from that comes insight and maybe, if we stick with it long enough, wisdom. Experiential learning then is defined here as learning in which the learner is in direct contact with the realities being studied or practiced to achieve a level of competence in a particular skill or knowledge domain. Such learning may begin as "unintentional" learning; that is, we may not be intentionally "studying" or "practicing" in the formal sense of these words. Rather we may begin our learning by chance—something catches our attention or needs doing or prompts us to seek answers to questions we never before thought to ask.

From this initial impetus we begin to explore new areas of learning—whether in our personal, professional, or avocational lives—and begin to achieve new skills, knowledge or understanding. Gradually, at our own individual rates, we begin to acquire the competencies or level of mastery we need—to enhance our work, our relationships with others, or other facets of our lives.

Throughout our lives, experiential learning serves to propel or motivate us to acquire new skills, knowledge and understanding. Sometimes, of course, the focus of our learning is intentional. We might take a training course offered by our employer, enroll in an adult education course at our local high school, hire a tutor to help us speak French, or seek new learning in any of a variety of ways. And, of course, in a great many instances, the two forms of learning merge. Take, for example, the man who discovers quite by chance that he has a green thumb. He might well take courses at a local adult school or spend time talking with or even working with people in a local garden center to focus his learning more specifically. He might also use the resources of his local library and read books or watch films pertinent to his interests. Such is the way almost all of us learn: sometimes in a highly focused manner and sometimes a bit haphazardly.

In this context, the question is often raised, "What about reading books?" In **learning** to read, there is no substitute for the experience of beginning to recognize sounds and words and eventually actually going through the process of gleaning meaning from the written word. Yet for most of us, be we geologist, dancer, electrician, elected official or parent, reading itself has been largely mastered and, unless we are learning a new language, is no longer a form of experiential learning. Rather it is a critical aid required for historical and theoretical understanding and often serves to stimulate reflective learning and integration.

From quite a different perspective, that of the college classroom, we often take experiential learning for granted. Can you imagine a biology course without a laboratory component or a public speaking course without oral exercises or a course in painting that included no painting? The question is silly, of course, but the point must be made that as teachers almost all of us build into our classroom work some experiential learning.

I believe that most college faculty see the relevance of experiential learning to their classroom instruction. They just don't name it so. Even many of the faculty who are involved with internship programs don't at first see the internship opportunity as "experiential learning" per se. But by any name, we regularly provide students or learners with an opportunity to come into direct contact with the phenomena being studied or the skills being practiced.

We did not invent the notion of experiential learning nor certainly were those of us in the nontraditional educational movement the first to see its relevance to human achievement. As is discussed by Houle (1976) there are strong philosophical and historical roots to the notion of experiential learning, early references to which can be traced back to the second century B.C. in China and carried forward through the centuries to such modern day thinkers as John Dewey and Piaget.

What we are concerned with here is the application of experiential learning to the curriculum of higher education.

We want to focus on the assessment of peoples' prior learning—those "achievements which have been acquired up to the point where an individual begins the assessment process" (NCVA, 1987)—most of which will have been acquired experientially. In colleges and universities all over the United States people are having their learning assessed in light of the academic standards set by groups of college faculty who recognize that learning does and will occur outside the confines of their own college classrooms. In assessing a student's learning, it is the faculty member's responsiblity to evaluate and equate the learning to that which would be expected as an outcome of a comparable college-level curriculum. It is to this task we now turn our attention.

Assessing the Learning

Although college faculty assess learning all the time in their classrooms, when it comes to assessing "prior learning" a certain mystique seems to arise, as if the process were separate from and infinitely more difficult than making traditional academic judgments about students. The purpose of this chapter is to take the mystery out of assessing prior learning and provide the reader with a variety of useful options for getting started.

To begin, though, it is important to remember that all evaluation or assessment requires human judgment. Even the most "objective" standardized examination is a product of human judgment. To one degree or another, the content and format of all questions and grading practices reflect the opinions and judgments of the test maker who must decide either alone or with others what is being tested and what is the acceptable or best answer. Regardless of how or when learning was achieved, the judgments of experts must be relied on if evaluations are to be made about students' achievements. What one hopes for in any evaluation is that groups of experts can agree to the criteria being set in the assessment process, and that there will be consistency among experts making independent judgments about those criteria or that students satisfying those criteria will be ready to master the next level of learning in that content area.

Put in other terms, what we look for in all assessment or evaluation, depending on the context of that assessment, is content validity, inter-rater reliability and/or predictive validity.

Seldom are traditional college faculty trained to think in these terms. Most often projects and tests are geared to the teaching, or input, the faculty member provides. Measurement is directed to the classroom experience provided. In some cases classroom evaluation may be based solely on the learning students may derive from one or two textbooks, with the students' grades being determined by a single final examination.

There are some who argue that classroom assessments are frequently capricious. No doubt we have all heard student discussions that went something like this:

> **Student 1:** We didn't even get through the entire syllabus and he tested us on the whole thing: 40 true/false questions, five short answer questions and two essays — all in two hours!
>
> **Student 2:** Well, we got through everything in the syllabus, but you should have seen her exam: one single essay question. It was weird; I wasn't sure what she was looking for.
>
> **Student 3:** At least you got to write. Our final examination consisted of 100 multiple choice questions, many of which didn't seem to have any right answers to me.
>
> **Student 4:** Gee, I finished my exam last week. We had a take-home final that I handed in Monday.

Like it or not, these are perceptions of the ways assessment is handled at many institutions. A department draws up a single syllabus on the basis of which all faculty are expected to teach but which relies on individual instructors to devise their own teaching and assessment methods. And just as teaching methods vary, so do the overall assessment methods of college teachers, even when, in contrast to the student perceptions simulated above, there is a departmentally-devised final examination. Most faculty still make judgments based on a variety of information provided by the student — both formally and informally — over the course of a semester. Even when teaching derives from the same syllabus, students earning the same institutional credit for American History 101, for example, may be exposed to different information, perceptions, historical interpretations and equally different assessment techniques throughout the term. Yet at the end of each semester when grades are posted and academic credit awarded, it is assumed that the institution has put its seal of approval on the learning achievement of every student who obtained a passing grade. The individual differences that can be ascribed to instructor variations in teaching and assessment are rapidly forgotten as are the differences in student achievement, since no two students can know or do know the same things, even if they receive the same grades from the same instructor.

For most classroom evaluations, faculty make up written and oral exams, assign and grade book reports, research papers, and special projects. In performing arts, science and other courses, they evaluate students' products and performance ability. Faculty create simulations and role plays; they rate students' oral presentation skills; and, of course, in most classrooms, a variety of techniques are used to make judgments about students' abilities and accomplishments. In American colleges and universities it is also not uncommon for faculty to weigh "attendance" and "attitude" when calculating students' grades.

Learning Outcomes[1]

Just as in classroom situations, the assessment of students' prior learning requires that academic judgments be made about what a student knows and can do. But by contrast with much current classroom assessment practice, before such judgments can be made, it is essential in assessing prior learning that the **learning expected for credit be defined** and that the **criteria for success be clearly articulated**, for in this situation, the teacher is not and cannot be responsible for providing the input to the student's learning. He or she must consider the discipline as a whole and determine what is most important, at what level the learning should be, and how best to assess the elements of the student's achievement. While most teachers at all levels of education are comfortable outlining "the material to be covered or taught," what is necessary for good assessment is a description of what students are expected to know and be able to do in relation to the established curriculum. One way to provide this description is for the assessors (experts) to draw up statements of their expectations for a particular course or discipline. Known as "learning outcome statements," these statements provide guidance not only to the assessor in making his or her judgments, but also to the students who must aim to prove that they really do possess the skills and knowledge they claim. As neatly summarized by Mitchell (1987), "Assessment is about generating evidence and making judgments of an individual's competence, by comparing his or her performance against the established criteria."

A learning outcome statement specifies the knowledge, skill and/or attitude that a person is expected to acquire in a given curriculum framework, enabling both teacher and student to know in

---

[1] Several of the examples in this section have been adapted from J. Marvin Cook, *A Handbook on Clarifying College Learning Outcomes*. CAEL, 1981.

advance what it is that students are expected to know and be able to do. Learning outcome statements may look like the following:

> The dental assistant student should be able to describe the development of the facial and oral structures.
>
> The biology student should be able to construct a diagram of the complete digestive system.
>
> The sociology student should be able to describe examples of social norms.
>
> The history student should be able to use primary sources to analyze in a written report a problem in American history between 1890 and 1914.
>
> The vocal music student should select material for a balanced recital program.
>
> The mathematics student should be able to calculate measures of variation.
>
> The personnel management student should be able to plan and conduct an interview which is appropriate to a pre-defined purpose.
>
> The chemistry student should be able to critique the analytical methods used and present valid conclusions from the results obtained.

These examples serve to highlight the five essential characteristics of learning outcome statements. They should

1. Be unambiguous and readily understandable by both student and teacher;

2. Describe observable, demonstrable and assessable performance;

3. Contain action verbs which have relatively few meanings;

4. Be broader in scope than lists of specific tasks or skills;

5. Be applicable to skills, knowledge and understanding.

Contrast the following:

> **Example A:** The economics student should understand the basic tools used to measure the status of the nation's economy.
>
> **Example B:** The economics student should be able to explain both orally and in writing the basic tools used to measure the status of the nation's economy.

Which example is clearer? Which names observable, assessable performance? Which contains an action verb? Which will elicit a response applicable to skills, knowledge and understanding?

Clearly the response is B.

Look at a few additional examples:

Example A: The food science and technology student should follow hygiene procedures at all times.

Example B: The food science and technology student should maintain standards of hygiene consistent with public health regulations.

Example A: The data processing student should be able to use a database.

Example B: The data processing student should be able to create data file formats and output specifications.

Example A: The heating and refrigeration student should be able to put oil in a vacuum pump.

Example B: The heating and refrigeration student should service and maintain compressor equipment.

Example A: The music history student should appreciate 19th and 20th century music.

Example B: The music history student should be able to analyze and give concrete examples of 19th and 20th century music.

Example A: The business management student should become aware of the major characteristics of formal organizations.

Example B: The business management student should be able to identify the major characteristics of formal organizations.

In each case, Example B meets the five criteria listed above. Each of these examples appears deceptively simple. To write clear and useful learning outcome statements requires practice and patience. Even more, the development of learning outcome statements requires that the content area of a particular discipline be looked at not from the point of view of what we expect **to teach**, but rather from the perspective of what we expect students **to learn**.

Often in workshop settings, faculty members suggest that this method of describing learning is applicable to other peoples' fields but not their own. The arguments range from, "This is great for vocational areas, but not for my field which is English literature," to "In my field, chemistry, the learning is too complex to describe in these simple terms," to "Mine is a theory course (developmental psychology); we're not concerned with learning outcomes," to "Why should I bother with learning outcomes when the proof is how the student does in the cooperative education program I oversee?"

Yet in **every** discipline it is not only possible to define learning in terms of outcomes it behooves us to do so if we are to make judgments or rate students by assigning to them either a letter grade or a pass/fail designation. We need to know what our own internal standards are. These standards serve to form not just our own academic credibility but that of our departments and institutions as well. We also know from a variety of research, that students do better, are more motivated, when they know what is expected of them. (Knefelkamp, 1981) Once though, in presenting this as yet another argument for developing learning outcome statements, a faculty member said, "I don't want students to know what they are supposed to know; otherwise they will all pass the test and I'll have no standards in my class." It took several of this gentleman's colleagues to point out to him that the mere fact that a student knows what is expected of him or her is no guarantee that he or she is going to meet the standards of performance set by the instructor as reflected in the examination or assessment process. In addition, although as teachers we serve an important gatekeeping function, our primary role is generally that of student advocate.

In almost all training sessions, given enough encouragement and practice, faculty can and do manage to write excellent learning outcome statements. One psychology faculty member in Quebec summed up the reaction of many faculty when she reported, "I thought this learning outcome business was just going to help me with my adult students, the ones who learned outside my classroom. What I have found though is that by describing my course content in learning outcome statements, I have improved as a teacher and I'm seeing better — more complete — work from the students. The learning outcome statements permit me to recognize individual differences in a way I could not before. I also feel a lot more confident in assigning grades than I used to."

What does it take to write learning outcome statements? As pointed out in *Developing Learning Outcomes* by J. Marvin Cook, each learning outcome statement should define:

1. Who is to exhibit the performance;
2. What performance is to be exhibited;
3. What conditions, if any, are to be provided for the learner at the time of the assessment; and
4. What constitutes a minimally acceptable response.

Faculty often find it helpful to review various taxonomies as they begin to develop learning outcome statements. Among these are those of Benjamin Bloom (1956), Robert Gagne (1965, 1977) and David Krathwohl (1964). Each of these offers a different perspective.

Bloom's taxonomy focuses on six areas of cognitive ability (knowledge, comprehension, application, analysis, synthesis and evaluation). Gagne's looks at intellectual skills (discriminations, concepts, rules and problem solving). And Krathwohl offers a taxonomy of five educational outcomes (receiving, responding, valuing, organization of values, and characterization of values). Each of these taxonomies has its own particular applications and uses but, most importantly, each provides a unique way of looking at and describing learning. One need not use only one taxonomy or perspective. The important message here is that faculty begin to think about their disciplines and their courses in a new way, one that focuses on what is to be learned, not just what is to be taught.

Setting Standards

Having established a set of learning outcome statements for a course or a set of courses, we need now to look at setting standards. How is this task done? What approaches are there? An example of strategy can be taken from the realm of baseball:

After a particularly exciting game, three umpires were in the dressing room discussing how they had made their calls.

The first one said, "I call it like I see it."

The second one said, "I call it like it is."

The third one said, "What I call it, makes it what it is."

Each of these perspectives is real and each is representative of faculty perspectives in making academic judgments:

Learning scores: assessors :: Baseball scores: umpires

Imagine three different faculty members. The first recognizes that what is being applied is an internalized standard, not explicitly spelled out, but, one hopes, applied with reasonable consistency: "I grade it like I see it."

The second perceives the standard applied as a universal standard, which the grader perceives would be recognized and applied by all other competent and efficient colleagues in similar situations: "I grade it like it is."

The third recognizes that in the absence of a precise or universal standard, each decision as to whether the learner has or has not met the standard refines and further defines the standard itself: "What I grade it, makes it what it is;" or put another way, "what I grade it, makes the standard."

As academic referees, our decisions are usually more complex and have greater impact on the lives of individuals; but the process nonetheless is similar to that which confronts the umpire. Of course, for most of us the setting of standards is an amalgam of all three situations. There is the expectation that our standards would be applied by all other like-minded colleagues, tempered by an element of "gut reaction", leading to a regular redefinition of the standard each time we assess the work of another learner. Just like umpires we need to learn our jobs and strive to do them consistently and fairly over time. And more often than not, we would like to be right and have our colleagues agree with our decisions on a regular basis.

Clearly, not least for our own self-esteem and academic credibility, fairness and consistency are important objectives in standard setting. Clarity of perception is essential and can only enhance mutual understanding among colleagues. In addition though, if we can clearly express the desired learning objectives and the basis on which we make our decisions regarding successful performance *and* convey this information to the learner, the assessment process can be both more effective and efficient in the **overall learning process**. Obviously though, we need to ask what and how much individual learners know and can do. Certainly, not every student can know everything. How do we or the learner know what is enough?

Look at the following example (adapted from Knapp and Jacobs, *Setting Standards for Assessing Experiential Learning*, CAEL, 1981).

To pass Journalism 104, the student must prepare 10 articles that are satisfactory in five respects:

1. The articles must be factually correct.

2. They must be grammatically correct.

3. They must address the needs of the audience.

4. The writing must be clearly and logically organized.

5. The writing must hold the reader's attention.

These five statements of expected learning outcomes attempt to define with some degree of precision what the learner is expected to have learned and be able to do. But before accepting these, we would want to know if there were general agreement that these are the five key or most important learning outcomes required for a student to pass Journalism 104. That is, would a larger group of journalism professors endorse these five elements of the standard? Consider some of the issues.

In considering the learning of any individual, we need to be clear about why we are interested in the learning outcomes:

- Do we want to know whether the individual has obtained certain skills, knowledge and understanding? or

- Do we want to be able to predict the future performance of the individual? or

- Do we want to recognize what has already been achieved and predict what might be achieved in the future?

In other words, standards are set for some purpose and we need to be clear as to what that purpose is. Sometimes we are concerned not only with the "content validity" but also the "predictive validity" of the assessment process. Rarely are we concerned **solely** with what has been achieved. As part of the assessment process, we often draw inferences about an individual's performance and ability. We need then to be clear about the nature of the inferences that can be drawn.

For example, in assessing an individual's learning in Journalism 104, we might recognize that the individual had acquired certain basic skills in journalism. The natural inference is that these skills could be used to good effect in a variety of appropriate contexts. On the other hand, we might also need to ensure that the learner had acquired a mix of separate skills, knowledge and understanding sufficiently well to be able to progress to a new course which would further extend these skills to more complex situations, with a high probability of success.

Such an analysis might lead us to reappraise the projected learning outcomes. For example, in the example cited above, under certain conditions, outcomes #2 and #5 could be counter effective: The articles must be 2) grammatically correct; and 5) the writing must hold the reader's attention.

It is possible that a piece of writing which does not obey all rules of grammar might be more effective in holding the attention of certain groups of readers. How might the statements of expected learning outcomes be written to reflect this possibility?

With respect to the standards themselves, what criteria could be used to differentiate between those learners whose learning is adequate and those who have not as yet reached the required standard? For example, for learning outcome #2 the criteria could be very explicit with respect to spelling and punctuation; e.g., no spelling errors, conform to standard English punctuation, and so forth. But could one be so explicit about use of language, implied in learning outcome #3, that the writing address the needs of the audience?

Similarly, with respect to learning outcome #5, how does one set criteria for holding the reader's attention? Is it necessary to define the reader's reading skills or ability? Should the criteria allow the reader to pause for reflection? Would it be desirable to specify both the length of the piece of writing and the number of facts, concepts or points of view used within a given piece?

Each question touches on important issues. Clearly, if there is substantial variation between members of the faculty, the "standards" may be weak and not useful in the context of assessing prior learning. Similarly, excessive attempts to become more precise in defining what is required can be self-defeating. As more and more is written, there is an increasing possibility that what has been written will not be read or is too much to facilitate a common interpretation. It is necessary to accept from the beginning that there is no absolute standard, that all standards have tolerances and that in a given context, the level of consistency among judges may vary depending on many factors, one of which may be the relative importance of what is being assessed. However, it is essential to strive for high levels of inter-rater reliability, meaning that independent judges assessing the same material or performance would come to the same or similar conclusions.

To establish standards effectively, faculty or other experts in the same discipline need to determine the desired learning outcomes for particular academic subjects or courses and to develop the standards for success. Working from those goals, it is then possible to apply the criteria in a consistent and valid way.

Most often, working in small groups, faculty find that it is easiest to draw upon the strengths of the department to set the criteria or standards together, relying then on "content validity" to insure the "appropriateness" of the various decisions that need to be made. The process of developing agreed upon learning outcome statements can often lead to lively discussions and discourse about what is really important in a given field. Most of us, as teaching faculty, have our own particular interests and strengths and it is to those that we often teach. However, in working towards group consensus, it is often necessary for some people to give up their special interests. Most often though, properly trained faculty aiming at a predefined goal are often very surprised to see how quickly they can come to a consensus about learning outcomes and standards. One faculty member, the head of the philosophy department at a large private East Coast institution, recently told me that going through the process of determining learning outcomes and standards for the courses he taught had made him "look at what was really important in philosophy in a way (he) hadn't thought about in 20 years." What strikes faculty immediately about this process is that it is student oriented, not teacher oriented and that it is learning that is critical to the educational process, not necessarily the teaching. By looking at curriculum in terms of "outcomes" rather than "inputs", we are better able to judge what it is we want students to learn and to know if and when they have actually achieved the learning.

An excellent example of this process in action in a large-scale system can be seen from recent developments in Scotland. In response to concern that young people and large numbers of adults were not properly prepared to meet the growing needs of business and industry, the Scottish Education Department (SED) in 1983 implemented an "Action Plan" which called for the development of a competency-based, modular system of education at the secondary and non-advanced further education levels. Groups of teachers, lecturers and industrial experts were brought together to work in small groups to determine the learning outcomes for a particular "module" (a 20- to 40-hour "course" in U.S. terms—LO2 or LO4) and the performance criteria or standards set for making sure students attained the expected learning outcomes. By way of example only, the working group for a module entitled "Wiring and Assembly Techniques" agreed upon these four learning outcomes:

The student should

1. prepare, join and terminate a conductor;

2. form cable looms to given requirements;

3. assemble and test an appropriate circuit or system to a given competent layout;

4. comply with regulations and procedures, and use safe working practices specified for the equipment and work area.

Corresponding to these learning outcome statements, the working group agreed to the following performance criteria (standards) by which students were expected to demonstrate their mastery.

The student will prepare a series of conductor assemblies in which:

a. joining and terminating methods are properly applied;

b. there is no damage to insulation or components;

c. the work is neat and accurate;

d. the assembly would function, if required;

e. the components are utilized correctly.

In addition, the working group specified additional performance criteria for specific learning outcomes:

LO2: The student will prepare a cable loom in which:

a. the work is neat and accurate;

b. the assembly is carried out correctly;

c. the assembly functions are required;

d. the correct components are utilized.

LO4: The student will:

a. wear all necessary safety clothing and equipment;

b. behave in a manner appropriate to the working environment;

c. use tools and equipment safely.

Another example taken from the music "Vocal Skills" module provides yet an additional way to think about learning outcomes and standards:

The student should be able to:

1. Sing to a competent level;

2. Sustain a vocal line within a structure of more than two parts.

3. Translate the standard musical notation appropriate to vocal range;

4. Lead a small group of singers in a group rehearsal;

5. Present a rehearsal group piece in concert to an informal audience.

The performance criteria by which to judge each student's performance were also established:

In individual and group performance in a range of musical styles, the student will:

(a) achieve fluent performance within the appropriate vocal range using chosen indication or notation, incorporating a range in excess of an octave, three notes per bar using simple and elementary compound time;

(b) pay due attention to accuracy of pitch, rhythm, appropriate phrasing and breathing;

(c) demonstrate musical awareness and sensitivity to other group members;

(d) achieve fluency in the singing of a melody and in part singing;

(e) co-ordinate a rehearsal for performance in which he or she demonstrates an awareness of the appropriate tempi, dynamics, pitch, and stylistic requirements.

For learning outcome #5, there are these additional specific criteria:

The student will:

(a) make satisfactory arrangements (administrative, technical and musical) for the effective performance of the rehearsed piece;

(b) demonstrate through the performance, musical awareness and an understanding of the importance of:
  i.   accurate pitch;
  ii. accurate notes and rhythm;
  iii. phrasing;
  iv. tempi and dynamics;
  v.   stylistic requirements.

The development of these statements of learning outcomes and standards should enable both instructor and student — whether classroom or not — to know exactly what is expected and whether or not the outcomes have been achieved. It is important to recognize that while the above standards have been put into operation, they are not seen as ultimate statements; rather, in the light of experience they are subject to on-going review and revision.

In passing, it is worth mentioning that these "modules" do not stand alone in the Scottish system. They are part of a progression of learning opportunities, much in the vein of traditional U.S. course offerings and cover more than 2,000 areas in the liberal arts, business, and technical and occupational fields. Unlike U.S. courses, however, the Scottish modules are not time-based. Achievement is linked to learning, not to time spent in a classroom.

By defining the learning outcomes and standards for all courses or sets of competencies in a given discipline, assessors are able to assess individual performance according to the rate and level at which individual students learn. It is possible, for example, that a student may need to focus on the theory part of a given course, having adequately demonstrated competence in the applied area of the course or vice versa. Or it may be that a student has a range of skills and competencies over a wide range of courses but lacks the depth of understanding in one or two. Having this kind of diagnosis enables both students and their mentors or teachers to make more rational educational decisions about a student's future educational needs.

Approaching learning from this perspective also enables us to evaluate **and value** the different strengths individuals possess. As is mentioned above, no two people can know or do know exactly the same material. In any given classroom, there is a range of student ability. Similarly, as we assess adults' prior learning, we witness a range of competence and ability. One of the most difficult concepts to convey to faculty as they begin to assess adult students' learning is that of keeping in mind the idea of the "minimally competent student." In setting standards and making our evaluations or recommendations — whether in the form of letter grades or pass/fail — we need to remember that in traditional college classroom evaluations "D" awards still enable a person to go on to new work in the same discipline. Why then, do some institutions or faculty members arbitrarily decide that adult students need to be superior before making a positive credit recommendation? That this practice is followed strikes me as all the more surprising given that common institutional practice accepts "C" or in some cases "D" credits in transfer even though it is impossible for the accepting institution actually to know who taught that particular student, what the standards were that led to that "C" grade, or what the student actually knows. The credits may even be 10 or more years old, yet still they will transfer and permit the student to go on to more advanced work.

Finally, it is important to note that in assessing learning, we are speaking of all the college-level learning an individual possesses, regardless of how, when or where it was acquired. Although we use the term "prior learning" throughout this book, in doing a workshop in Quebec some years ago, the interpreter quietly asked me "How recent is prior?" The question took me by surprise but immediately I saw the difficulty with the phrase "prior" learning. Is not all learning prior in that the minute we have a thought it is by its very nature relegated to a past moment? Given the human capacity of recall, perhaps we should use the term "present" learning, or maybe we should simply think of "learning" as we have suggested in formulating the title of this book. What we are interested in assessing and crediting is learning, college-level learning, regardless of how, when, or where it was acquired. Adults, just as the other students in our classrooms, have a vast array of skills and competencies and it is these—regardless of the name we assign to them—that we are interested in assessing. (At one point, we had considered using the term "extra-institutional" learning to describe non-college classroom learning until a training director of a large company said, "Extra-institutional? We just built a $2,000,000 training facility. I hardly think the learning our employees undertake is extra-institutional!")

If we think about assessment in the context of the learning of the traditional classroom student, can we be certain that the effective learning displayed by our students during assessment is a direct result of our teaching, guidance and stimulation? Indeed, I think we would hope that at least some of the learning has resulted from self-motivated efforts. What we do not know is how much of the displayed achievement has come from undirected learning either in parallel to or prior to the taking of our course. It is possible in some situations that the learning has had little to do with faculty input. What the assessment reveals—including good classroom assessment—is what the student knows and can do, not the method of, or stimulus to, the learning (Debling, 1987).

In assessing adult students' learning then, it is essential that we keep in mind that each will possess a range of skills and knowledge. If learning outcome statements are in place and predefined standards have been established, it is then possible to assess those skills and this knowledge in light of our expectations. Some students will know and be able to do a lot; some only a little. In either case, we will have the basis for making rational judgments about each student.

In summary then, there are many advantages to developing and using a learning outcome system with clearly articulated standards:

1. faculty can make valid and reliable judgments over time;

2. students can know what is expected of them and measure their own achievement;

3. students need not repeat what they already know;

4. faculty experts, whether as assessors or instructors, can know in advance on what basis to assess existing learning and facilitate new learning;

5. faculty can accurately monitor learners' progress in the light of specific learning attainments, not just symbolic grades;

6. the assessment process can be independent of the method of learning.

In the next chapter we will see how the stipulation of learning outcomes and performance criteria also enable us to determine more readily the appropriate assessment method to be used for each student and for different kinds of learning.

References

Bloom, B.S. (Ed.), Englehart, N.D., Furst, E.J., Hill, W.H., and Krathwohl., D.R. *Taxonomy of Educational Objectives — The Classification of Educational Goals, Handbook I: Cognitive Domain.* New York: David McKay Company, Inc, 1956.

Cook, J.M. *A Handbook on Clarifying College Learning Outcomes.* Columbia, MD: CAEL, 1978.

Cook, J.M. *Developing Learning Outcomes.* Columbia, MD: CAEL, 1978.

Debling, G. "Assessing Occupational Competence." Working paper, Sheffield, England: October 1987.

Gagne, R.M. *The Conditions of Learning.* New York: Holt, Rinehart and Winston, Inc., 1965. 1977.

Houle, C.O. "Deep Traditions of Experiential Learning." In M. Keeton (Ed.), *Experiential Learning: Rational, Characteristics, and Assessment.* San Francisco, CA: Jossey-Bass, 1977.

Knapp, J. and Jacobs, P. *Setting Standards for Assessing Experiential Learning.* Columbia, MD: CAEL, 1981.

Knefelkamp, L. "Translating Student Development Theory Into Practice for Student Affairs Professionals." University Park, MD: University of Maryland, 1981.

Krathwohl, D.R., Bloom, B.S., and Masia, B.B. *Taxonomy of Educational Objectives — The Classification of Educational Goals, Handbook II: Affective Domain.* New York: David McKay Co., Inc. 1964.

Mitchel, L. "Assessing Occupational Competence: What Does It Mean In Practice?" Working Paper prepared for Scottish Vocational Education Council, Glasgow: 1987.

National Council for Vocational Qualifications. Report of APL Working Group, London: 1987.

Scottish Vocational Education Council. Module Descriptors, Glasgow: 1986.

Stecher, C. "CLEP and The Great Credit Giveaway." *Change*, March 1977, Vol. 9 (3), pp. 36–41.

Susan Simosko *author of Earn College Credit for What You Know, has served CAEL both as a member of the central staff and as a consultant. She recently formed her own business in Sheffield, England and provides training, assessment and evaluative services to organizations in Great Britian, the United States and elsewhere. Her address is 20 Chorley Drive, Sheffield, England Sl0 3RR.*

Chapter 2
Assessment Techniques

Susan Simosko

While learning outcomes and standards are critical components of the assessment process, by themselves they often seem quite removed from student learning. Early on in workshop settings faculty most often want to know exactly what it is that they will be assessing and how they will actually do it. It is on this question that we now focus our attention.

First and foremost it is essential to remember that it is **learning** that is being assessed, not experience, and that it is the student's responsibility to convey this learning or competency and not just reiterate the experiences from which the learning was drawn. Students can and do convey their learning in a variety of ways but quite commonly at colleges and universities across the country, students are expected to construct a "portfolio" of their learning, a documented portrait of what they know and can do. In many situations, the portfolio is enhanced by other forms of assessment—performance assessment, product evaluation, written and oral examinations, simulations, and so forth. "The assessor's task is to judge a candidate's behavior (or performance) and decide whether it meets the (established) standards." (Mitchell, 1987). There are many ways this result can be achieved.

Student Preparation

Generally speaking the construction of a portfolio requires that the student go through four distinct, inter-related processes:

1. Identifying the learning.
2. Expressing it in terms of college-level curriculum or competencies.
3. Relating it to overall educational and career objectives.
4. Compiling the evidence or demonstrating competence.

Actual procedures vary from college to college but most colleges expect students to follow a set of guidelines roughly formulated around these steps. Some colleges offer "portfolio development" courses or workshops to help students through the process; others provide self-instructional materials for students to follow. Almost always, colleges provide counselors or advisors to provide guidance and support to students as they begin the process.

To identify their learning, students are usually asked to begin with their experiences — to review and write down all those critical events and activities in which they have been engaged: work experiences, both paid and unpaid, avocational interests, homemaking and other special skills. They may list books they have read, travel experiences they have had, religious or political projects in which they have been involved. They may mention noncredit courses, training programs or independent study projects — any significant learning experience.

Following this step, they are then asked to describe and identify the learning that resulted from these experiences. Put another way, students are asked to look at the outcomes of their own learning. For example, a person who served as treasurer of her local school board might describe a portion of her learning as:

- I can prepare annual budgets for a school district with an annual budget of $3 million and have done so for the past six years;

- I can follow and meet state and federal auditing guidelines;

- I can give public presentations;

- I can prepare accurate fiscal reports; and

- I can work well with others.

Students are then usually asked to consider their learning in light of their overall educational and career objectives. This is an important step because often adults seek credentials in areas other than those in which they have already attained competence or success. For example, counselors often encounter talented women who have worked as secretaries for a number of years but who want to change direction — move into the field of data processing or management or self-employment. So in spite of the fact that a woman may have many assessable skills and competencies generated from her employment as a secretary, they may not be those that would be most helpful to her academically in reaching her new educational and career goals. She would not, therefore, necessarily seek an assessment of all of her skills and competencies as a secretary. On the other hand, some of her skills and abilities — her business writing, for example — may well be assessable and applicable to her new chosen academic program.

Some students also identify areas in which they have a high level of attainment but in areas that cannot be credited **per se** for college credit. One student for example enrolled at a large midwest university, was a Master chess player. He had a very high level of skill, knowledge and understanding, but could not earn college credit directly for these competencies. He was, however, able to earn credit for his knowledge of game theory and a number of other related, transferable skills that were applicable to the curriculum of his institution.

Identifying the learning and considering its application to overall educational and career objectives is a critical phase in the early stages of the assessment process. For this reason, students should receive as much support and encouragement as possible in this process.

Evidence of Learning

Students are often most eager to begin with the evidence of their learning: the certificates, letters, awards, and other products of their learning — just as was Barbara Tilton, the hypothetical woman described in the introduction of this book. And indeed, those are the artifacts from which faculty assessors may begin to make their judgments about the student's learning. But it is only at the last stage of developing the "portfolio" that students turn their attention to the evidence of their learning.

It is important to reiterate that in all cases what is assessed is learning. The materials or products produced by the student serve more like a road-map to the student's accomplishment and effort. The documents or products are not assessed or evaluated in and of themselves, but rather serve as the documented evidenced of the student's learning. They are used and evaluated by the assessor in light of predetermined learning outcomes and standards.

Most prior learning assessment programs expect students to write a narrative or autobiographical sketch of themselves in which they highlight the significant learning experiences, express what it is they know and can do and offer some sort of index to the materials being provided in the "portfolio." Each college or university develops its own procedures and policies, but the materials received by faculty as part of the assessment process are as unique as the very nature of human endeavor.

In presenting evidence of their learning, students may offer either **direct** or **indirect evidence** or some combination of each. Direct evidence refers to those products or performances actually produced by the student. Poems, paintings, computer programs, dress designs, architectural drawings, written manuals, a video tape of the student dancing or playing a musical instrument, or an actual performance — these are all examples of direct evidence of the student's learning. Examples of indirect evidence may include a magazine review about the students' poems or paintings, a letter of verification from an employer attesting to the student's accomplishments in preparing company training manuals, the program notes of a concert in which the student performed or photographs of completed dresses or buildings that the student claims to have designed. The lists in both the direct and indirect categories are endless. It is up to the assessor to determine in conjunction with the student the best way for the student to present the evidence or proof of his or her learning.

In some cases, students will have no visual evidence of their learning. Take, for example, the avid reader who has become an independent scholar on William Faulkner. He or she has read the primary works and many secondary sources but has never written a paper, given a lecture or led a class discussion about some aspect of Faulkner's work. Such a person would still be an excellent candidate for prior learning assessment. In the portfolio narrative or autobiography the student might provide an annotated bibliography of the books she has read in order to provide the assessor with an indication of the depth and breadth of her learning. The assessor might then set up an interview with the student, ask her to write a paper on a particular topic or give an oral presentation on a selected topic. There are many ways to assess students' learning other than, or in addition to, relying on the evidence they submit in their portfolios.

At most colleges and universities, students have a variety of options in presenting themselves. But it is important to remember that the faculty assessor also has options and indeed a responsibility to develop appropriate assessment methods to insure that the student meets the articulated academic standards or learning outcomes. The assessment process, therefore, requires the use of expert judgment in a variety of ways. In an earlier CAEL publication, *Expert Assessment of Experiential Learning — A CAEL Handbook*,[1] Richard R. Reilly suggested seven functions of the expert judge. These have been adapted below.

1. Define Criteria. As described in Chapter 1, the expert should play a role in the specific definition of the standards against which the evidence presented by the student is to be judged. These standards should be as explicit as possible.

2. Select the Assessment Method. In some cases the assessment procedure may be predetermined by the institution or chosen by the student. In many cases, though, once the criteria have been specified, the expert will need to decide or select which type of assessment procedures is most appropriate for eliciting the most relevant sample of behavior, performance or other evidence. In making this decision the expert may, in fact, be able to take advantage of existing assessment procedures that could be adapted and structured for a particular student with relatively little revision.

3. Structure the Assessment. The degree of control over the structure of the assessment process that an individual assessor has will vary according to the situation. Structure may be imposed by others involved in the assessment process, for example. But in many situations, it is the assessor who decides which methods will be used in the assessment; e.g., a review of the materials in the portfolio; an oral interview, a simulation, a written exercise, and so forth.

4. Adapt the Assessment. The expert assessor can have considerable impact on the validity of the overall judgments made by adapting the assessment technique to the experiences and needs of the individual. Adaptation does not necessarily imply a lack of structure, but rather the selection of the fairest and most relevant technique(s) for the demonstration of a student's particular learning or competence.

5. Observe the Assessment. The expert must observe a student's behavior, performance or products in light of the established performance criteria. It is impossible for an assessor to make his or her judgments about an individual's competence without direct observation of the student's external evidence or behavior.

---

[1] Richard Reilly, et. al., *Expert Assessment of Experiential Learning — A CAEL Handbook*, Princeton: NJ, 1977.

6. Judge the Learning. The most critical function of the assessor's role is, of course, the act of judging or quantifying the student's learning. The expert must consider the evidence that has been presented, perhaps eliminate what is irrelevant, weigh what is relevant, and finally balance this against the established criteria or standard. In most college and university assessment programs assessors have three options in making their recommendations: to award credit, to deny credit, or to request additional information from the student.

7. Record the Results. It is critical to the academic credibility of the assessment process that the assessor's observations and judgments be recorded and maintained for a specified period of time in keeping with the current institutional practices at a given college or university.

Techniques

Product Assessment

Product assessment is one of the most common and direct ways of evaluating students' learning. Products lend themselves directly to the evaluation of skills and knowledge. Clearly, product assessment is inherent to the assessment of learning in the fine and performing arts. Paintings, pieces of sculpture, photographs, musical compositions, films or tapes are just a few of the many examples that could be cited. However, by way of example only, letters, memorandum, articles, training manuals and other documents related more to the business world may similarly be considered products of the students' learning, in this case in the field of business or management. So too with technical skills, scientific achievements, and human services work: models, laboratory or research reports, and case histories also can be viewed as valuable products of students' learning. Most fields of human achievement yield products.

Some distinctions need to be drawn between performance assessment and product assessment. In the former, the student actually performs live for the assessor or assessment team. In the latter, the assessor or assessment team receives the **end product** and uses that to make judgments about the student's learning. For example, in undertaking a performance assessment for a music composition course a student may be asked to play her compositions directly for the assessor. But it may be more practical and expedient for the student to submit a copy of her manuscript with a tape of her work.

In this instance, an important issue is raised about product assessment, namely that of authenticity. How, if a student were to submit a tape of her compositions, could the assessor be sure that it was indeed the student's work? In a classroom situation, faculty come to know students over the course of the semester. But in assessing adults' prior learning at some colleges and universities, faculty may never directly meet with the student. But there are several ways in which authenticity can be verified. Students may submit letters of verification from their instructors or employers to accompany their products. Or the assessor may himself set up an in-person or telephone interview with the student to ask specific questions about the work. Students are usually quite open and willing to discuss their products of achievement, so assessors should have little or no difficulty in verifying the authenticity of students' work.

Another important issue in product assessment is "process." As Ruth Churchill points out in *Expert Assessment of Experiential Learning*, "While the product can testify clearly to some of the learning, . . . other learning associated with the process by which the product came into being needs to be evaluated in other ways. For example, in evaluating (the) ability to develop curricular materials, some learning is implicit in the unit itself — for example, (the) ability to set objectives for students, to select materials, and to evaluate changes in student behavior. Equally important process learnings are not explicit — for example, how the student identified the problem initially, how she gained the background needed to work on it, how she evaluated the success of what she attempted to do. Here both the product and the student's account of how she produced it (may) be needed."[2]

One last distinction that needs to be noted is that between product assessment and indirect documentation. Students often present newspaper clippings, job descriptions, certificates and other such materials as evidence of their learning. Seldom can these types of evidence stand on their own as adequate proof of the student's learning. Newspaper clippings, for example, may have been press releases prepared by the student himself; job descriptions convey only what a person is supposed to do in a job, not what he or she actually can or does do; and certificates, if we do not know the nature of the certifying body itself or know about the requirements that led

---

[2] Ibid.

to the successful awarding of the certificate, do not convey what it is a person knows and can do. In conjunction with other assessment methods, including the presentation of products completed by the student, documentation can be helpful in rounding out the picture a student presents of him or herself. It can also serve as stimulus for additional inquiry by the assessor.

Conducting Product Assessments. In general, there are five steps that are undertaken in conducting product assessments. Again, there may be variations from college to college but most include some aspect of each of these:

1. **Set learning outcomes and standards.** In undertaking any product assessment, the student's work needs to be directly linked to the learning outcomes and the standards set for success in a particular course or set of courses. Some products may stand by themselves. A set of poems, for example, published by the student in "The New Yorker" may serve as sufficient evidence for earning credit in a creative writing course. Other products, like an annual report for a retail company, may represent only partial evidence of the student's learning for a course, say, in retail management. Other products may need to be supplied by the student or supplemented by evidence requiring the use of other assessment procedures. Again though, when the assessment is linked to specified learning outcomes and standards, the relevance and applicability of various products becomes very clear.

2. **Develop a checklist or form for the assessment.** While the learning outcomes and standards will serve as the basic guide through the assessment process, many assessors find it helpful to develop checklists or rating scales related to each of the learning outcome statements in order to evaluate the specific characteristics of products. The more clearly the check list or rating scale is linked to the observable learning outcomes, the more consistently and reliably the assessment can be made. These checklists or rating scales can also be useful to determine whether certain elements of the learning should be given more or less weight in the assessment process.

3. **Prepare students.** Students need to be given sets of guidelines so that they know the criteria by which their products will be evaluated. Giving students copies of the learning outcomes and the standards is often sufficient, although use of the checklists by the students can be extremely helpful as well in developing their evidence.

4. **Prepare evaluators.** Faculty assessors, just like students, need to have access to and understand the learning outcomes and

standards by which products are to be evaluated. This is especially true if more than one assessor is to be used. Often one or two group training sessions with the faculty to be involved is adequate. Frequently at the beginning of a prior learning assessment program, a small group of faculty is involved. As the program expands new faculty are brought on board without the benefit of adequate training or instruction. This omission can lead to inconsistent standards and indefensible judgments. It is critical, therefore, that all faculty involved in the process be regularly and consistently trained to use the learning outcomes and established standards when undertaking a product assessment.

5. Plan assessment. As is mentioned above, sometimes a product or set of products cannot stand alone as adequate evidence of a student's learning. It may be that the assessor will want to hold an interview with the student, ask for additional products or a written paper, or view an actual performance by the student. As early as possible, the student should be told what he or she will need to do. That goal requires prompt and careful planning by the assessor. One caveat, as again pointed out by Ruth Churchill is: "There is the danger that ability **to verbalize** about the skills involved in (the production) of a product may not be the same as the ability **to make the product** and in the interview or paper some students may be rewarded for verbal skills rather than for those for which they are presumably being evaluated."[3]

Performance Assessment

Performance assessment, like product assessment, is frequently used to assess adults' prior learning. Unlike product assessment, however, in which the outcome itself is used to evaluate the students' learning, in performance assessment, it is the process itself, the act of doing, which is considered. There are two general categories of performance assessments, each with a number of variations: "prepared performance" and "simulated performance."

The assessment of a prepared performance is generally useful in evaluating a student's learning in the performing arts — music, dance or theatre arts — or in areas of physical education. Learning outcomes are generally set to relate to technical or physical skill,

---

[3] Ibid.

level of competence, artistic renditions, and so forth. In this situation, the student prepares for and actually performs in front of the assessor or the team of assessors and the assessor makes his or her judgments about the student's learning on the basis of the performance.

In the assessment of a simulated performance, the assessor endeavors to create a situation reflecting the real-life one in which the student claims competence. Such simulations are useful in assessing a wide variety of skills and abilities in fields as diverse as allied health, management, sociology, psychology, auto mechanics, chemistry, biology, aviation and so forth. Although simulations are designed to be representative of real life situations, they are usually **by design** controlled — either for reasons of expediency, economy or safety, or some combination of all three and as such cannot fully represent the gamut of issues and problems the student may encounter in the "real" situation. Simulations therefore, must be prepared with great care and with a full understanding of what is to be assessed.

Some examples of simulated situations designed for assessment purposes include:

1. A dental hygiene student working on the teeth of a model.

2. The management student undertaking an "in-basket" exercise.

3. The sociology student analyzing and responding to a number of case histories.

4. The auto-mechanics student repairing a portion of an engine.

5. A clinical psychology student conducting a simulated interview.

6. A chemistry or biology student performing certain laboratory procedures under controlled situations.

7. An aviation student completing a set of assigned manuevers in a stationary, simulated cockpit.

These are just a few examples of the way in which simulated performance assessment can be conducted. It is critical to the success of this method of assessment that to the extent possible, the simulation reflect a range of real-life characteristics and that, again, the assessment be geared to specific learning outcomes and performance standards which both assessor and student know in advance.

Since it is often not feasible or desireable for assessors themselves to observe students' performance in real-life situations, some consideration might be given to training an employer or supervisor to do the assessment. Often it is these people who are most familiar with, and perhaps best qualified to judge the actual performance of adult students. It is quite possible that in the not-too-distant future the links between academic instructors and industrial employers will be strengthened in the growing call for "national standards" in some occupational areas. Ideally, it would be desireable in some fields for both the academic and the industrial experts to jointly develop learning outcomes and acceptable standards of performance with each assuming responsibility for the assessment of the student. Such a system, while it may seem foreign to American readers, has been established with some success in Great Britain (Ellis, 1987).

As with product assessments, it is conceivable that further information will need to be obtained from the student in the form of a piece of writing, through an interview or some additional assessment technique. The nature of the area being assessed, the scope of learning of the student and the learning outcomes and standards will also play an important part in determining the sufficiency of the performance assessment by itself. The assessor together with the student will need to consider these various factors in planning to conduct a performance assessment.

In their chapter, "Performance Assessment," Arnold Fletcher and John L.D. Clark,[4] develop a series of questions in five key categories that may be helpful in planning and conducting a performance assessment. What follows has been adapted from this chapter in *Expert Assessment of Experiential Learning — A CAEL Handbook*, edited by Richard Reilly.

1. **Establish learning outcomes and performance criteria.**

    a. What are the crucial behaviors involved in the performance? Are some more important than others? Should they be weighted?
    b. Is sufficient information available about the student's ability?

2. **Choose the best assessment method.**

    a. Can a real-life situation be utilized or would a simulation situation be more appropriate?

---

[4] Ibid.

b. Is there a cost factor to be considered?

c. If a simulation is to be created, what are the critical components that need to be designed? Is adequate equipment available? Are the physical arrangements proper?

d. Which is more appropriate, product or performance assessment, or both?

3. **Stipulate the assessment process for all who are to be involved.**

a. Have appropriate criteria been established to select assessors properly?

b. Have adequate plans been made to insure proper observation and record keeping?

c. Have necessary scoring procedures and forms been set up, such as checklists, rating scales, etc.? (See above under "Product Assessment".)

d. Can one expert do the assessment or are multiple raters preferable?

e. Are all assessors appropriately and adequately trained?

f. Are procedures in place for checking the reliability of the assessors periodically?

4. **Develop good administrative practices.**

a. Have instruction and guidelines been established for the students?

b. Have necessary assessment controls been established, including desirable physical conditions, sequence and timing of activities, for example?

c. Have security or confidentiality controls, if necessary, been put into place?

5. **Consider the financial implications of performance assessment.**

a. Is the validity and reliability of the assessment worth the high cost? (For example, would it be cost effective for an assessor to go to a concert to see the student conduct a professional orchestra or would a simulation be sufficient or would appropriate documentation (indirect evidence) be adequate?

b. Is the field changing so fast that a particular assessment situation will soon be outmoded?

c. Will there be enough call for the simulated situation to warrant its development?

These are just some of the questions assessors will want to ask and answer as they begin to develop and conduct performance assessments.

As in using any assessment method, teams of faculty or experts will want first to define the learning outcomes and establish the performance criteria or standards. Having accomplished this task, the actual assessments themselves—whether from real-life or simulated situations—will enable the students and the assessors to understand better the level of learning that has been acquired.

Interviews and Assessment

Interviews of one sort or another are used throughout a person's college career, indeed, throughout one's life. Interviews can help us to exchange information, verify information, influence or change behavior, diagnose problems, or serve any number of other purposes. The interview can be used in different ways during the assessment process.

Often at the very beginning of the assessment process, an exploratory or "counseling interview" may be undertaken between the student and an advisor or counselor. The primary purpose of this interview is to determine the areas of strength that may be applicable to the student's attempt at seeking credit and/or to motivate the student to begin the process. A counseling interview may also be used to help prepare the student for a panel interview or some other aspect of the assessment process. Principally, interviews of this sort are designed to influence the student's behavior in a positive way. Although part of the overall assessment process, these interviews are not designed to assess the student's learning in order to make a credit determination. A strong distinction needs to be drawn between the counseling interview and the interview designed by the assessor to evaluate or verify the student's learning.

There are three ways that interviews are regularly and successfully used by assessors to judge students' competence: one, the oral examination, is designed to assess skills and knowledge directly; the second, usually a less structured interview, is designed to supplement other means of assessment, such as product or performance assessment; while the third is used to verify documentation provided by the student.

An oral examination is an interview, usually highly structured, in which questions are planned in advance and relate directly to the competence being assessed. Often pre-set standards determine the assessment decision regarding the student's competence. Oral examinations are used in fields like medicine to determine certification and licensing, and in fields like counseling, where interpersonal competence is assessed. The oral examination is a relatively objective demonstration of competence or knowledge. It provides an opportunity for the examiner(s) [assessor(s)] to judge the manner and content of the reply to a direct question or to ask for clarification or justification for information previously obtained. It is often used in conjunction with performance assessment. Oral exams are often time-consuming and therefore costly, but as noted in earlier CAEL research (The CAEL Validation Report, Chapter IV, by Warren Willingham and Associates, 1976) are reliable and valid assessment tools.

A very structured one-on-one interview makes use of a "schedule" — a list of specific questions to be asked in a predetermined order. In a semi-structured interview, the interviewer knows exactly what information will be solicited but varies the wording and sequence of questions for maximum effectiveness with individual students. In the least structured interview, the assessor determines in advance the areas or topics to be covered but varies the questions according to the specific situation and/or student.

In some assessment situations, students are interviewed by a panel of assessors. Although this may be a highly anxiety-producing situation for students, it may be less time consuming than a series of one-on-one interviews and in some situations the panel can also serve as a simulation in which the student must work with a group. Panel members need to take care that the interview does not become a "trial by jury." Just as in other assessment situations, the preparation of the panel interview needs to be thorough and careful.

A less common type of oral assessment is the leaderless group discussion, used most often to assess leadership or other group dynamic skills. In this situation, a number of students are brought together and asked to discuss a topic and/or assume a particular role within the group. The assessor(s) does not enter into the discussion, but rather observes and evaluates according to pre-defined criteria.

These types of oral assessments are most useful, obviously, in obtaining direct information from a student about his or her skills and knowledge in a particular field. The nature of the third kind of interview, to verify documentation submitted by the student, will be determined by the material itself and the particular situation. Frequently though when a student has had an employer write on his or her behalf, describing the work responsibilities, the performance level of the employee, etc., an assessor may still require additional detail. Often a few well directed questions can serve to validate a student's learning expediently and effectively. In this vein, an assessor may occasionally wish to get in touch with an employer directly too. Permission to do so should first be obtained from the student unless the employer indicates in the letter that he or she has discussed the possibility with the student and would be pleased to provide additional information verbally in a telephone conversation.

Developing the Interview. As in the other sections of this chapter, there are five recommended steps that should be taken before conducting an assessment interview.[5]

1. **Establish learning outcomes and standards.** This step, which must be more than obvious to the reader, is essential for any assessment. Experts need to determine the levels of competence in the specific area to be assessed and write clear and unambiguous learning outcome statements and standards.

2. **Develop the content of the interview.** Once the learning outcome statements and performance standards have been established, the interview questions or schedule need to be designed. They should relate directly to the expected learning outcomes and established standards. Questions should enable the respondent to cover the subject matter thoroughly and should be an appropriate mix of varying difficulty.

3. **Develop observational and recording procedures.** A procedure for recording and rating students' responses should be developed in advance of the interview. A rating scale or check list, with space provided for comments, is often most helpful. The use of such a recording instrument is especially important in a leaderless group discussion. In all cases, of course, the rating scale should be closely tied to the expected learning outcomes and the performance standards.

4. **Pilot the interview.** All questions, materials and rating scales should be tried out with a small sample of students and with more than one judge. This step will allow ambiguities to be cleared up and

---

[5] This section has been adapted from "The Interview and Related procedures by Judith Pendergrass, Jane Porter Stutz and Richard Reilly, *Expert Assessment of Experiential Learning — A CAEL Handbook.*

unnecessary questions dropped. Every attempt should be made to insure that the interview questions elicit responses that are adequate and relevant to the standards.

5. Develop the final product. A final set of questions or discussion topics, guidelines for administration, and a form for recording should be produced. In the case of a leaderless group discussion, a set of background materials for students should be included.

Although the actual questions will vary significantly from field to field and from situation to situation, some general categories of questions may prove helpful to assessors as they begin to consider their interview schedules. These might include asking the student to:

1. Recall activities or successful events and evaluate their significance.
2. Draw comparisons between and among learning experiences.
3. Analyze issues, events, or the student's own strengths and weaknesses.
4. Demonstrate problem-solving skill within a given context.
5. Identify trends or systematic changes.
6. Identify and apply particular theories or practices to given situations or circumstances.
7. Evaluate or critique a particular situation or product using internal and/or external evidence.
8. Formulate a plan of action based upon a given case history or set of circumstances.

These are only a few of the strategies that have been found useful in developing interview schedules. A great many books and articles have been written on the "art of interviewing." The interested reader should have little or no difficulty finding ample theoretical and technical advice on how to further develop reliable and valid interview schedules. Readers may also find one or more of the taxonomies listed in Chapter 1 helpful as they begin to frame their ideas for developing questions for the interview assessment.

Assessment of Writing

In many respects direct written work produced by the student is similar, if not exactly the same, as other products developed by the student. If a student, for example, is seeking credit in English composition, he or she would expect to produce and submit written evidence of his or her competence in English composition. The assessor, in turn, using the defined learning outcome statements and standards, can evaluate the student skills and knowledge of English composition. In the same vein, poetry, short stories, novels, technical reports, and other forms of writing can be assessed.

The difficulty comes when students are asked to develop bibliographic essays or narratives and these come under the scrutiny of the assessment process. Many students who are highly skilled and knowledgeable in some areas of learning, say music, auto mechanics, or chemistry, may in fact have underdeveloped writing skills. Their essays about themselves may sound immature and may even be fraught with errors. What to do? Should the writing about experiences and learning be considered an inherent part of the learning and therefore subject to evaluation, or is it possible, even preferable, to judge the subject matter skill and competence as a separate, complete unit for assessment?

College faculty and other experts are divided on this issue. Some argue that the ability to do a task or to show evidence of college-level learning, such as playing a musical instrument at professional level, should be judged as an independent unit. Since writing in a performance course usually requires no writing **about** the learning, why should adult students be treated any differently? In other words, why should their initial essays about themselves be considered part of the actual material that is assessed. In this example, strictly speaking, the ability to write is not one of the learning outcomes expected in musical performance and therefore the portfolio essay or narrative, while of some interest — much as some information faculty learn about their classroom students is of interest — cannot be considered as part of the assessment process.

This argument holds true not just in performing arts disciplines, but in many professional and occupational areas in which expected outcomes of a particular subject area do not include writing per se. It is the argument of many faculty that while the ability to write well should indeed be an outcome of a college education, writing is a separate skill that should be taught or assessed by writing experts, not by those who are specialists in mathematics, aviation technology or dental hygiene.

Other faculty or experts would take strong exception to this argument. They would stress that a student's ability to describe and analyze his or her learning in writing is critical to the learning process itself and therefore, should very much be a part of the assessment process. And in fact, at many colleges and universities, students are expected to demonstrate writing competence across most of their subject matter courses. And in that idea lies the key to making a decision about whether or not to include the students' portfolio essays as part of the assessment process: **if the expected learning outcome for a course or a discipline includes demonstrating writing competence at varying levels, then indeed the written portion of the portfolio should be subjected to evaluation,** and the student advised accordingly. If this expectation is present, then criteria must be established by which the written material can be fairly and reliably assessed. However, if the ability to write well is not part of the expected learning of classroom students in a particular course or set of courses, then the assessment of the writing in a student's portfolio may not fairly be part of the assessment for that course or set of courses.

Does this view mean that the narrative or essay portion of the portfolio has no value? Hardly. Such written work often has significant value both to the student and the assessor. For students the written work can help to integrate the entire learning experience and provide a clearer perspective on where he or she has been and where he or she wants to be educationally, professionally and personally. And for assessors, the written material can serve as a road map to the student's learning, helping to raise questions about the documents or products being submitted or clarifying some particular learning experience the student may have had.

Using the narrative or essay in this way, as a road map to the student's learning, suggests certain caveats, however. In many prior learning assessment programs students are required to write long biographical essays which are frequently included in the portfolio. In these essays students may tell of their childhood experiences, painful experiences they may have had in adolescence, the death of their parents, or their bitter experiences with a divorce. While these experiences may have served as critical turning points for a student, it is important to ask: Is this knowledge of a person's personal history relevant to the learning that is to be assessed? Is knowing the pain a person experienced as a child in any way related to her skills and competence as a bank manager? Is knowing that a person is very active in a particular church or political party in any way related to his competence as a librarian? Can knowledge of these personal tragedies and activities in a person's life affect the outcome of an assessment? We'd like to think not, of course, but there is idiosyncratic evidence to suggest otherwise.

On more than one occasion, I have used a portfolio sample from a student who was active in a particular church. Although the student was seeking credit for his knowledge of the political process in American government, in his biographical essay he spoke a great deal about how the church influenced his home and family life and how, after a long struggle, his personal values had emerged out of his religious convictions, eventually leading him to further his education. Although the student also spoke of how he had come to learn about the political process in American government and had ample evidence to verify a good deal of his learning, faculty reading over this portfolio example have had very mixed reactions to it. Some start sighing in the middle of reading the essay, saying, "This annoys me. I don't want to know all this business about his church activities." Others get angry, allowing their own values to come into conflict with those expressed in the essay. Still others, taking the "objective" route, skim over the material, looking for the material directly relevant to the course being considered.

Again the question must be asked: What is it that we need to know to assess a person's **learning**? If we are not assessing experience, why must we know the personal details of a person's life? Is knowing the motivating factors or the pivotal transitions in a person's life or his or her belief system relevant to what he or she knows and can do? If so, how can we articulate the expected learning outcomes and standards? Do we expect to gather and know this type of information from our classroom students?

On the other hand, is the essay an indication of the integration of the student's learning? Can we define the criteria by which to judge it as a piece of college-level work? Should an English department faculty member assess it? Or should a well-trained counselor or student advisor assess it, looking for the development of interpersonal growth and problem solving ability? Or should, in fact, the content area specialist evaluate it as part of the student's total learning?

Would a narrative statement directly related to the student's learning and spelling out what the student claims to know and be able to do be sufficient? Should the narrative provide a review of the material presented for assessment? Can one narrative statement cover more than one course (assuming the courses are in the same discipline) or is a separate one needed for each course?

These are questions that must be answered **before** a prior learning program can be established or an assessment properly undertaken. All too often students are asked to perform certain difficult and complex tasks — like writing a lengthy autobiographical essay — without knowing in advance the purpose such a piece of work will play in the assessment process.

It may be that these essays, often so critical to the student's learning, best be used in the reflective stage of the assessment process. However, regardless of the role the essay is to take in the assessment process, the reader may wish to review the general considerations proposed by Miller in *Expert Assessment of Experiential Learning — A CAEL Handbook,* 1977:

1. **Determine the specific factors on which the student is to be assessed before making any judgment.** Make sure that the student has a clear understanding of exactly what factors (e.g., writing competence, substantive knowledge in some area, etc.) are to be assessed.

2. **Obtain a representative sample of the student's writing.**

    a. If the assessment is to be based on prior written work, provide guidelines to the student so that a representative sample of writing related to the criteria can be assessed. If a student claims to have written 20 short stories, for example, the assessment should be based on more than one or two.

    b. If the assessment is to be based on a requested writing sample, the criteria and guidelines to the student should be clear and relevant to the factors established.

3. **Prepare for assessment.**

    a. Through committee action or other methods, standards should be established. A file containing samples of acceptable levels of student work can be set up (and used for training purposes).

    b. Clear guidelines should be established for judges so that they know exactly what factors are to be assessed.

    c. Through workshops and/or practice sessions, judges should be trained to use the agreed-upon procedures and standards.

4. Complete a final assessment report.

   a. Clear guidelines should also be provided for the writing of a
      final assessment report. The report should clearly relate the
      assessed material to the learning outcomes and the pre-
      established standards.
   b. Whenever possible have at least two judges read the mate-
      rial. Neither judge should know the other's evaluation prior
      to doing his or her own assessment of the material.
   c. As a rule, judges who are personally familiar with the writer
      should not be used. Whenever possible, the student author
      should remain unidentified.

Other Assessment Tools

As Jacobs and Gulliver discuss in the next chapter, there are
numerous other tools that can be used to evaluate students' prior
learning. Special mention needs to be made of licenses and certificates, often submitted by students in their portfolios as evidence of
their college-level learning.

Certain licenses and certificates can be extremely helpful in
indicating a student's skills and knowledge. Many do serve as valid
evidence of a student's college-level learning. Possessing an FAA
Mechanic's Certificate with Airframe and Power Plant Rating, for
example, enabled a student at one East Coast college to earn 55 academic credits for courses such as Basic Electricity, Aircraft Electrical
Systems, and Engineering Drawing. Similarly, possession of a current real estate or registered nurse license often enables the student
to be awarded credit on the basis of that license.

These forms of documentation can and often do reflect, beyond
a doubt in the minds of many experts, that the holders of these credentials really do possess learning equal to or greater than that
reflected in a particular college curriculum. Implicit in the automatic
credit recommendation is an understanding on the part of the faculty at a given institution of the training, rigor and standards
demanded of the holder of the license or certificate.

In many respects, licenses and certificates — when the standards are known and accepted as being college level — are a bit like
a student's transcript from another accredited institution. Although
the faculty at College A may not know the exact professor a student
had or even the course outline of Biology 101 at College B, for example, they will assume the standards of a "C" or better would be com-

patible with their own standards and accept the student's grade in transfer. Although licenses and certificates do not come with grades, many enable experts familiar with the standards to recognize possession of particular ones for credit.

Under no circumstances, however, should a certificate or license be used to make a credit award unless the standards are known and there is evidence that the student has met the criteria by a reliable assessment process. Many certificates and licenses are awarded on the basis of attendance or interest and do not reflect in any way an individual's skill or competence. Certificates from industrial training programs may be useful **indications of possible learning**, but without additional information, cannot stand alone as sufficient evidence of the student's learning.

Summary

Obviously in undertaking the assessment of adults' prior learning, there are many different possibilities and techniques. The process lends itself to infinite variation and creativity for both students and assessors. The assessment of prior learning provides an opportunity to consider what is important not only in a given discipline or academic course but also in a person's life. Whether the assessment includes products, performances, interviews, written work or the evaluation of indirect evidence, always the focus is on outcomes — what the student knows and can do.

It is critical that in undertaking the assessment process the faculty or expert judges are not only familiar with their fields, but are open to considering outcomes, not just the inputs they provide in their classroom instruction. It is essential that they grapple with the often difficult decisions that are necessary to write learning outcome statements and to arrive at appropriate criteria or standards for success. They must also be fully accountable for the procedures and policies they apply during the assessment process and maintain accurate and verifiable records of their assessments. The assessment of adult students' prior learning can provide a rich and exciting professional learning opportunity for the assessor as well as for the student.

References

Churchill, R. "Product Assessment." In R. Reilly, *Expert Assessment of Experiential Learning — A CAEL Handbook*, Columbia, MD: CAEL, 1977.

Fletcher, A. and Clark, J.L. "Performance Assessment." In R. Reilly, *Expert Assessment of Experiential Learning — A CAEL Handbook*, Columbia, MD: CAEL, 1977.

Miller, M. "Assessment of Written Material." In R. Reilly, *Expert Assessment of Experiential Learning: A CAEL Handbook*. Columbia, MD: CAEL, 1977.

Mitchell, L. and Johnson, C. "Selecting Suitable Methods of Assessment." Working Paper prepared for MSC/NCVQ Technical Advisory Group, Glasgow: September 1987.

Pendergrass J., Stutz, J.P., and Reilly, R. "The Interview and Related Procedures." In *Expert Assessment of Experiential Learning — A CAEL Handbook*, Columbia, MD: CAEL, 1977.

Reilly, R. (Ed.). *Expert Assessment of Experiential Learning — A CAEL Handbook*, Columbia, MD: CAEL, 1977.

Willingham, *The CAEL Validation Report*. Princeton, NJ: ETS, 1976.

Susan Simosko author of Earn College Credit for What You Know, has served CAEL both as a member of the central staff and as a consultant. She recently formed her own business in Sheffield, England and provides training, assessment and evaluative services to organizations in Great Britian, the United States and elsewhere. Her address is 20 Chorley Drive, Sheffield, England S10 3RR.

Chapter 3
Using Examinations to Award Credit for Prior Learning

Paul Jacobs and Kate Gulliver

In this chapter we explore the use of examinations to award credit for adults' prior learning. First we discuss some general considerations, then turn to particular categories of examinations.

General Considerations

The End-Of-Course Examination

As is mentioned in an earlier chapter in this book, a college faculty uses a variety of means to assess learning: classroom participation, term papers, examinations during the course, and end-of-course examinations. In some instances, the entire assessment of learning is carried out through a single end-of-course examination. Such examinations are also sometimes used to assess claims of extracollegiate learning equivalent to that of a course or courses.

The major considerations in using an end-of-course examination are:[1]

1. The test should provide reasonable coverage of the entire course.

   The test should cover all the important topics, or select them so that performance on the sample will reflect what

---

[1] Course challenge examinations are developed on the assumption that the course for which the examination is developed is the appropriate standard. However, see page 56 on the need for more generic examinations. Sometimes, moreover, the focus of assessment may be on aspects of a course other than "its content;" e.g., upon reasoning processes acquired.

the student would be able to do on a test that does cover all the important topics.

2. The minimum passing score should reflect sufficient mastery of the course.

A particular student's score can be compared to the scores of other students. This is called norm-referenced measurement and requires that judgments be made on the basis of the performance of a group of students.

Alternatively, a student's score can be compared to a predetermined standard. This method is referred to as criterion-referenced measurement and requires that a passing score be predetermined. Those earning grades above this point pass; those below do not. Classroom instructors commonly use one or the other of these methods.

3. The examination should be secure.

To prevent students from having access to the examination before they are tested, it is common to develop a new examination each time the course is taught, or to rotate the use of multiple forms of the examination.

The End-Of-Course Examination Without a Course

The next logical step is to conceive of an end-of-course examination without a course: the source of learning is not necessarily classroom instruction, but the student's own experiential learning or self-directed study. Testing in the absence of instruction is not a new idea; examinations of one kind or another have been used for admissions screening, licensure, and job screening for many years.

In this situation, all the above considerations apply, as well as some others:

1. The examination should be in an academic area in which the college is willing to give credit.

An institution's transfer of credit policy may suggest a guideline here.

Credit for courses previously taken at another accredited college or university will be accepted upon the recommendation of the appropriate departmental chairperson. In general, students may expect to receive credit for a course which is the same or almost the same as a course given at State University and which they have passed with a grade of 'C' or better.

'Blanket credits' may be granted by a department for an acceptable course for which there is no precise equivalent at State University. (Blanket credits are not creditable toward specific requirements, but are applicable toward a total number of credits required for the degree. Some colleges call these 'free elective' credits).

2. The examination should be valid for the intended purpose.

Most educators and many laypersons urge that "an examination must be valid." Psychometricians, however, will add " . . . for the intended purpose," since validity is not an inherent quality of an examination. An examination valid in one set of circumstances may not be valid in another: an end-of-course examination valid at one college may not be valid at another, depending on institutional standards. Validity, in this usage, is a matter of the test's actually measuring what it is intended that it measure—in this case the learning which the learner claims to have achieved and which the examiner deems appropriate and adequate to the proposed designation of the credits.

Current Practices

Often examinations are the easiest form of prior learning assessment to get accepted by faculty, since they resemble most closely what faculty already use in assessing students. Most colleges now accept standardized proficiency examinations in some way, and most offer the option of departmental challenge exams to advanced learners.

Recently, written examinations have received considerable attention from educational psychologists and psychometricians. The literature on written examinations, however, contains comparatively little material pertinent to the assessing of prior learning.

Categories of Examinations

Departmental Challenge Exams

A college may offer a "challenge" examination that allows students to demonstrate they have already mastered the material in a particular course. This demonstration is generally for one of the following purposes:

> to grant credit for the course;

> to excuse the student (without credit) from taking the course, thereby recognizing that the student meets a particular degree requirement or meets a prerequisite requirement for a more advanced course;

> to "validate" a request for transfer credit for a similar course taken elsewhere; or

> to diagnose the student's knowledge for appropriate course placement.

In an innovative program Metropolitan State University makes use of challenge examinations for **diagnostic** purposes. Adult students with experiential background are given a brief examination to decide whether they should:

> apply for credit for a course because they already appear to have the necessary theoretical and practical knowledge;

> take a special theory-only course because they already have the practical knowledge; or

> take the traditional course in the area.

There are a number of academic and administrative issues that need to be addressed in offering challenge examinations. The importance of each of the following issues will depend on the purpose of using these examinations.

Generality of policy. Will challenge examinations be offered for every course offered at the college? Will challenge examinations be offered for courses given at other accredited institutions but not offered at your college? Can the policies concerning challenge examination be uniform across departments and courses?

"Locus of control." Will the examinations be developed, administered and scored

> by a college-wide Office of Testing?

> at the departmental level? or

> by individual instructors?

"Openness" of the challenge. May a student merely fill out a simple form to apply to take a challenge examination or must the student show "probable cause" that he or she has mastery of the course material? If so, what must the student do?

Timing of the challenge. May a student apply to take a challenge examination at any time in his or her college career, or only during the first year of enrollment?

Publicizing the availability of challenge examinations. Will the opportunity to take challenge examinations be mentioned in the college catalog? Will faculty and staff be aware of this possibility and encourage students to take advantage of it when appropriate? Will all policies concerning challenge examinations be conveniently available in written form to students?

Preparation for the challenge examination. Are there descriptive statements, reading lists, past examinations, course outlines, etc., that a student may consult before deciding to apply for a challenge examination, and in preparing for such an examination?

Payment for the examination. Will the student pay a testing fee? Will the student who passes pay an additional fee for "posting" the credits onto a transcript? Will the total fee to the student equal the tuition fee for the course, allowing the student to save time and effort but no money?

Recording of results. Will the examination be graded pass or fail, or in terms of letter grades? Will a record of failure be placed on the student's transcript? Will the result, if in terms of a letter grade, be included in the student's grade-point-average?

Appeals. Will the student have access to an appeal process in case of failure or misunderstanding?

Re-taking an examination. Will a student who fails have an opportunity to re-take the examination?

The examinations themselves. Who develops a challenge examination? If five different instructors teach different sections of the "same" course, will there be five different challenge examinations for it? What is the format of the examination (written; oral)? If written, is it essay or multiple-choice? If essay, who grades it? According to what standards? How is the passing score determined?

Current practices regarding these issues vary tremendously among colleges. If the intention is to **encourage** students to take challenge examinations as a way to award credit for prior learning, then regardless of how other issues are resolved, the college should:

feature the availability of challenge examinations in a clearly delineated section of the college catalog, and make sure they are cross-referenced in the catalog index under "examinations for credit," "departmental examinations," "challenge examinations," "credit for prior learning," etc.;

be sure faculty and administrative staff are aware of the examinations and support their use; and

have written statements of policies regarding challenge examinations that may be distributed to students by the Registrar, Departmental secretaries, the Testing Office, the Office of Adult Learning Services, the School of Continuing Education, and so forth.

Standardized Credit by Examination Programs

History. One of the first organized applications of the concept of credit by examination in the U.S. was the **Advanced Placement Examinations,** introduced by the College Board and administered by Educational Testing Service (ETS) since 1955. As the name implies, the purpose of the Advanced Placement Program (APP) was and is to allow able high school students to be assessed for advanced placement into college study.

In 1963 the New York State Education Department established the **College Proficiency Examination Program** (CPEP) as the first credit by examination program oriented toward the nonclassroom learning of adults. The philosophy of credit by examination is summed up well in an early slogan of the CPE Program that "what you know is more important than how you learned it." This program is now called **Regents College Examinations.** Outside of New York State these tests are known as **American College Testing Proficiency Examination Program (ACT PEP)** tests, and are administered by the American College Testing Program.

Building on the CPEP model, in 1965 the College Board, with administrative support from Educational Testing Service, introduced the **College Level Examination Program (CLEP).** CLEP is one of the two most used credit by examination programs in the United States. It offers two sets of examinations, the Subject Exams and the General Exams.

- The 30 to 50 Subject Exams reflect individual college course subjects in the arts, sciences, and business.

- the five General Exams, as their name implies, are broader, less course-specific tests which cover material taught in humanities, social sciences, natural sciences, mathematics, and English courses, usually during the first two years of a traditional college program.

Another popular program is the **DANTES** series of Subject Standardized Tests (DSSTs). DANTES, the Defense Activity for Non-Traditional Educational Support, originally developed these examinations for use by military personnel only. Today, however, they are available to civilians as well. The DSSTs in the arts and sciences and business are similar in subjects and credit value to other exams. In addition, there are a number of DANTES titles in technological and occupational areas.

Taken together, the APP, ACT PEP, CLEP, and DANTES batteries offer over 150 separate standardized examination titles in the arts and sciences, business, nursing, computer science, education, technology and occupational areas.

Development. The development of standardized proficiency examinations involves a partnership between college faculty and the respective testing agency. The faculty, as the subject matter experts, are responsible for determining the content and the skills to be measured. The testing agency assumes responsibility for constructing the tests and for assuring the psychometric legitimacy of the examinations. In these large national testing programs, faculty must have appropriate academic credentials and current teaching experience in the discipline of the respective examinations. Most testing agencies are pleased to provide or publicly print the names of the academic men and women who construct their tests.

The process of objective test development begins with a definition of the subject area to be addressed, and the development of a detailed content outline or set of content specifications. In this part of the process, faculty must resolve the variations in the teaching of a subject from one college or curriculum to another. To serve a sufficiently large and varied body of test-takers and institutions, an examination must be as "generic" or universal as possible.

Once details of the test content are agreed upon, "item writers" (usually college faculty) develop a large number of potential test questions or items, each one keyed to a particular section of the content outline. This pool of test items is reduced and edited into a final body of questions that is determined to test the specified content. Often pretesting can supply additional useful information about the items that improves the quality of the final forms of examinations.

The resulting examination is then administered to a group of learners (such as college students just completing a comparable course) who can be expected to have adequate mastery of the content. On the basis of their performance, a set of normative standards for the test is established, and from these standards a scoring scale is developed.

For those aspects of college subjects that are difficult to assess through multiple-choice questions, essay or extended-response questions are frequently used. Clear criteria are established for what constitutes a good, fair, or poor response to such questions. Essay responses are a required part of some nationally sponsored examinations and are centrally graded by specially trained college faculty. In the CLEP program, optional essays are available with the Subject Examinations. If required by the college or university, the essays are sent to the receiving college to be graded by their own faculty.

College faculty and administrators may usually obtain inspection copies of standardized examinations. Procedures for review range from a testing agency staff member's handcarrying examination copies to the college to registered mailing of the examinations in sealed envelopes. Strict security procedures are required, and inspection of the tests is usually limited to particular members of the college community for a limited amount of time.

Each college may decide on the minimum passing score it will require for acceptance of an examination. Many follow the recommendations developed by the American Council on Education (ACE). There are three major approaches colleges have taken in determining acceptable or passing scores for CLEP Subject Examinations at their institutions:

1. Under the administration of ETS, a reference group of college students drawn from a variety of different kinds and geographically diverse locations has completed both relevant courses and the corresponding CLEP examinations. The end of course grades are submitted by the participating institution along with the completed examinations. After statistical analysis of the data, the mean scores are provided for "A," "B," and "C" students. Most colleges award credit at the mean "C" level for each examination following the ACE recommendation.

2. Another group of colleges award credit to students whose scores exceed 50 percent of the scores in the reference group mentioned above.

3. Some colleges develop their own local norms and set their own passing scores for each examination on the basis of those norms. Most testing agencies can provide information on how to perform these tasks.

What follows is pertinent information for each testing program discussed above:

Advanced Placement Program

Available to: Anyone in the United States.

Courses covered: Exams available in 13 areas including Art, Biology, Chemistry, Computer Science, English, French, German, History, Latin, Mathematics, Music, Physics, and Spanish.

Dates available: May. Instruction available only through high schools. Test registration date set by Educational Testing Service.

Preparation: Descriptions of content of each test available (purchase only).

Examination charges: Payment in advance, not refunded if examination is failed.

Recording of results: Numerical Score (1-5).

Re-taking an examination: No limit—offered only once a year.

For further information: Advanced Placement Program, Educational Testing Service, Princeton, New Jersey 08541.

Proficiency Examination Program

Available to: Anyone in the United States, special arrangements outside the United States.

Courses covered: Over 40 titles in the arts and sciences, business, nursing.

Dates available: Test administration in October, November, February, March, May, June. Most tests given at three administrations per year. Registration required five weeks in advance.

Preparation: Study guides free of charge for all tests. These include test objectives, content outline, bibliographies, and sample questions.

Examination charges: Payment in advance, not refunded if an examination is failed.

Recording of results: Varies from exam to exam: Pass or Fail, numerical score, or letter grade.

Re-taking an examination: Exams may be retaken after 60 days. Candidates must re-register and pay the exam fee.

For further information: ACT PEP, P.O. Box 168, Iowa City, Iowa 52243. (In New York State: Regents College Examinations, Cultural Education Center, Albany, New York 12230.)

College Level Examination Program

Available to: Anyone in the United States. Special arrangements outside of United States.

Courses covered: Five General Examinations, 30 Subject Examination titles in History and Social Sciences, Foreign Languages, Composition and Literature, Science and Mathematics, Business.

Dates available: Every month except February and December. Students need to register four weeks before test date.

Preparation: Guide to the CLEP Examinations available. Includes description of each test, sample questions and suggested resources for preparing for each exam (purchase only).

Examination charges: Payment in advance, not refunded if test is failed.

Recording of results: Numerical score.

Re-taking an examination: Must wait six months before retaking test. Must pay another test fee and submit new test application.

For further information: College Level Examination Program, Box CN 6600, Princeton, NJ 08541-6600.

DANTES

Available to: Any United States resident.

Courses covered: Examinations in Science, Social Sciences, Business, Applied Technology, Languages, and Mathematics.

Dates available: Depends on organization offering the examinations.

Preparation: Guide to the examinations available, includes description of each test, sample questions and suggested resources for preparing. No charge.

Examination charges: Payment in advance, not refunded if examination is failed.

Recording of results: "Pass or fail" grades are issued. Only passing grades become part of the test candidate's permanent record.

Re-taking an examination: Must wait six months before retaking it. No limit on the number of times tests may be retaken.

For further information: DANTES, Educational Testing Services, Princeton, New Jersey 08541.

Examinations as Part of the Prior Learning Assessment (PLA) Process

Under certain circumstances examinations can play an important role in the prior learning assessment process.

The student may claim learning for which no objective evidence is available. In other cases the student may present evidence which is insufficient to justify the awarding of credit. In either situation any of several testing options may be appropriate vehicles for documenting the students' learning.

The choice of an examination will depend on several factors: the subject of the assessment, the particular content to be tested, and the degree to which it corresponds to that of the college curriculum, and the nature of the learner himself or herself.

In many cases, however, standardized examinations do not exist that would fairly or comprehensively assess the student's learning. The alternative used by most colleges is a faculty-made examination tailored to the individual student. The process itself, as is discussed in a previous chapter, can range from a written examination which is a modified form of an end-of-course test to an oral interview exam. In most colleges the examination, like the assessment process itself, is based directly on the content of a course in that college's curriculum.

The form of the examination determines to a large extent what it tells about the learner. The more open-ended the examination, the more likely it is to demonstrate the range of the individual's learning.

A course-based written test, for example, will measure the extent to which a student has mastered what is commonly taught in a particular classroom.

An oral examination tends to be more open-ended than a written one, since the examiner can, through follow-up questions, allow the student to demonstrate knowledge over a wider range of subject matter than a predetermined set of questions will allow.

Advantages worth noting:

This type of test has greater potential for bridging the gap between the largely theoretical content of college curricula and the practical orientation of many adult students' learning.

An oral examination can also measure the student's ability to articulate his or her learning and to respond to questioning.

Some practitioners of assessment by portfolio do not regard testing as a necessary component of the process. They believe that the documentation, product or performance presented in the portfolio should stand on its own merits as evidence of the learning. Some academic departments, however, prefer that an examination, written or oral be a part of the prior learning assessment (PLA) process.

An oral examination, appropriately designed, allows the assessor to focus on the student's learning rather than on the college curriculum. A test of this kind can measure the student's ability to communicate his or her learning coherently and to relate it to an academic discipline. The ultimate outcome, though, is generally credit defined in terms of recognized college subjects. Depending on the format and orientation of the oral exam, it may or may not test mastery of detailed factual content as thoroughly as can a standardized, paper-pencil examination.

College or University Developed "Standardized" Examinations

Challenge examinations may differ for the same course within the same college in terms of content, format, scoring standards, and conditions of administration. A "standardized" examination, by contrast, attempts to keep content, format, scoring standards, and conditions of administration as comparable as possible from one test candidate to another. This effort is made in order meaningfully to compare one candidate's score with those of others or with a predetermined standard. Standardization is accomplished by:

providing a detailed manual of administrative procedures;

establishing specifications for acceptable free-response answers;

reviewing the agreement among different scorers; and

comparing a candidate's score with

the distribution of scores of others who have taken a course similar to that which the examination corresponds to, or

a minimum passing score established by a consensus judgment of experts.

The three programs described below, Thomas A. Edison College Examination Program (TECEP), Ohio University, and New York University (NYU) Language Examinations, have taken the latter approach.

A number of colleges and universities have developed programs of examinations for credit for prior learning for their own students, and have also made them available to students registered at other institutions. One way that these programs differ from national programs of standardized examinations-for-credit (such as CLEP) is that passing of their examinations automatically entitles the student to credit at the institution offering the examination, rather than being a recommendation for credit that may or may not be acceptable to a particular institution. Examples of three such programs are given below.

The Thomas A. Edison College Examination Program (TECEP)

The Thomas Edison State College Examination Program (TECEP) is Edison's own examination program. Originally designed especially to help enrolled Edison State College students meet degree requirements, the examinations are now administered nationally and may be used at many other institutions.

The TECEP program includes the DANTES Subject Standardized Tests. These tests, originally designed to provide credit opportunities to U.S. service men and women, are now available to the civilian population as well.

Available to: Any United States resident

Courses covered: Over one hundred subjects in Liberal Arts, Business, Professional, and "free-elective" areas.

Dates available: Once a month; registration required four weeks in advance.

Preparation: A Test Description Book that contains an outline of topics, sample questions, and list of recommended readings for each examination is available at a cost of $10.

Examination charges: Payment in advance, not refunded if examination is failed.

Recording of results: "Pass or fail" grades are issued. Only passing grades become part of the test candidate's permanent record.

Re-taking an examination: An examination may be repeated, subject to these restrictions:

> The candidate must wait three months before retaking it.

> Only one retake is permitted.

> To retake an examination, one must re-register and pay the appropriate fee.

For further information: Office of the Registrar, Thomas A. Edison State College, 101 West State Street, CN 545, Trenton, New Jersey 08625.

The Ohio University Course Credit By Examination Program

Available to: Any United States resident.

Courses covered: Over 100 subjects in Liberal Arts, Business, Professional, and "free-elective" areas.

Dates available: Once a month; registration required four weeks in advance.

Preparation: At registration a brief syllabus containing a short course description, a list of the required textbooks and information on the nature of the examination are issued.

> The Independent Study program of Ohio University offers two options: students may prepare for and take an examination completely on their own; or, if they feel they need the help of a professor, they should consider an Independent Study course by correspondence or an Independent Study project.

Examination charges: Payment in advance, not refunded if examination is failed.

Recording of results: Letter grades of A to F are given. Failures are reported to the Office of Student Records and will appear on students' records. A pass-fail option is available.

Re-taking an examination: May be repeated after six weeks, with instructor's approval.

For further information: Independent Study, Tupper Hall 302, Ohio University, Athens, OH 45701-2979. In Ohio, call toll-free 1-800-282-4408. In continental U.S. outside of Ohio call toll-free 1-800-342-4791.

The New York University Proficiency Testing in Foreign Languages

Available to: Any United States resident.

Courses covered: Arabic, Chinese, Danish, Dutch, French, Gaelic, German, Modern Greek, Hebrew, Hindi, Italian, Japanese, Korean, Norwegian, Persian (Farsi), Polish, Portuguese, Russian, Spanish, Swedish, Thai, and Turkish. Five basic areas are tested: comprehension of the spoken language; oral questions with written responses; the written language in a free composition; translation from the native language into English; and translation from English into the native language.

Dates available: Twice a month at New York University; registration at least one week in advance. Once a month at Thomas A. Edison State College in Trenton, N.J.; registration required four weeks in advance. By arrangement at select military testing sites.

Preparation: Brief statement available from New York University.

Examination charges: Payment in advance, not refunded if examination is failed.

Recording of results: Test candidate earns from 0 to 12 credits, depending on score and policy of college/university receiving the credits.

Re-taking and examination: No retakes are permitted.

For further information: Foreign Language Program, NYU School of Continuing Education, 2 University Place, Room 55, New York, NY 10003. (212) 598-3346.

Specialized Examinations in Professional Areas

Many colleges and universities use a student's possession of professional licenses and certificates as a basis for awarding credit for prior learning. Many of these professional licenses and certificates in turn are based upon some combination of work experience, instruction, and examinations. Here too, then, examinations play a role in the awarding of credit for prior learning.

The extensive range of professional licenses and certificates that are considered credit-worthy by many colleges is often a surprise to faculty members. Here is a partial listing of some widely recognized licenses and certificates:

>Chartered Life Underwriter (CLU)
Chartered Property Casualty Underwriter (CPCU)
Certificate in Data Processing (CDP)
Certificate in Computer Programming (CDP)
Certified Professional Secretary (CPS)
Certified Public Accountant (CPA)
Chartered Financial Consultant (ChFC)
FAA Air Traffic Control Specialist
FAA Airline Transport Pilot
FAA Commercial Pilot Airplane License
FAA Commercial Pilot Rotocraft License
FAA Flight Engineer
FAA Flight Dispatcher
FAA Flight Instructor Airplane Rating
FAA Flight Instructor Instrument Rating
FAA Flight Navigatorp
FAA Instrument Pilot Airplane License
FAA Instrument Pilot Rotocraft License
FAA Mechanic Certificate/Airframe and Power Plant Rating
FAA Multiengine Airplane
FAA Private Pilot Airplane License
FAA Private Pilot Rotocraft License
Registered Professional Reporter

The Registered Professional Reporter examination received credit recognition through the efforts of Dr. Harriet Cabell, Director of the New College External Degree Program at University of Alabama.

Listing of other licenses, certificates and training programs that are credit-worthy may be found in:

American Council on Education. *The National Guide to Educational Credit for Training Programs.* Macmillan, New York: 1986.

The University of the State of New York, State Education Department. *College Credit Recommendations: The Directory of the National Program on Noncollegiate Sponsored Instruction,* 1985.

Paul R. Jacobs *is the Director of Test Development and Research at Thomas A. Edison State College, New Jersey's college for adults. Previously he conducted research for nine years at Educational Testing Service. He has lectured widely in testing, prior learning assessment, and the improvement of thinking skills.*

Kate Gulliver *is Coordinator of Marketing and Communications for Regents College of The University of the State of New York. She is also a Regional Manager for CAEL Mid-Atlantic.*

Issues in Assessing Prior Learning

While the basic principles of good assessment are the same for all subject matter areas and levels of learning, over the years it has become evident that certain questions and concerns do arise that are often unique to particular groups of subject matter experts. In this section we have tried to highlight some of these issues to assist faculty and administrators in their efforts to anticipate concerns that may arise on their own campuses.

Each chapter focuses on a particular subject matter area, raising questions such as how much credit should be granted, when the assessment process should begin for a given student, or what can be done about some of the natural tensions in the process. The specific chapters cover issues in assessing the liberal arts, occupational and technical areas, business, the performing arts, and professional areas.

Each of these authors has been involved in the business of assessing learning for many years and, as such, has been an experiential learner in solving problems and looking for answers to difficult academic questions. All have worked with a wide range of faculty, institutions and students. These chapters represent some of their observations and inquiries into the specific subject matter domains of assessing adults' prior learning.

Chapter 4
Issues in Assessing the Liberal Arts

Susan Simosko and Graham Debling

For the best part of the past decade, if not longer, colleges and universities have increasingly been providing experiential learning opportunities for their traditional-aged liberal arts students. The Albany Semester Program in New York State, for example, encouraged students from many different kinds of educational programs to participate in full time, fifteen-week internships with State agencies (Brooks and Althof, 1979). Students from the humanities, social sciences and natural sciences were able to obtain valuable learning opportunities by working in museums, the office of Economic Development, the Department of Environmental Conservation and so forth. Similarly, colleges and universities have long encouraged junior year abroad programs, a semester of student teaching for those preparing for the teaching profession, and cooperative education programs for those wanting to experience or learn about particular professions or career paths.

In many different ways colleges and universities have sought to enhance traditional classroom learning in the liberal arts with work-based or other experiential learning opportunities. How is it then that so often we hear concern expressed by faculty and administrators that the liberal arts do not lend themselves to the assessment of adult students' prior experiential learning; that the liberal arts are based on theory and therefore not assessable except through paper/pencil tests; that learning achievements obtained through work or independent initiative are not relevant to the academic focus of classroom instruction?

This is not the place to argue the merits or meaning of a liberal arts education. Much has been written on the subject and widely discussed and debated in the national press—both professional and popular.[1] But this is the place to ask vital questions about the assessment of liberal arts learning regardless of how, when or where it was acquired. Consider the following:

John, a mid-level manager in a large industrial bank wrote and had published two historical mystery novels. When he decided that he wanted his degree at age 40, he applied to his local college seeking credits in aspects of British and American history, English composition and creative writing. His goal was to become a college instructor of writing.

Barbara, a full time secretary and single mother was active in a number of local environmental and political action groups. Over the course of two years she provided the leadership to one group in particular that eventually obtained the necessary State support to prevent the building of an environmentally injurious dam. At the age of 35 she sought credits in marine biology, environmental issues and political pressure groups. Her goal was to become a full-time paid lobbyist.

Louise, confined to a wheel chair since the age of 19, developed and trained others to use an exercise program for physically disabled children using childrens' literature and American jazz. She believed that a degree would enable her to round out her education and would add credibility to her work.

No doubt each of us knows or has heard about individuals like John, Barbara or Louise. They seem to accomplish the extraordinary using their own perhaps unextraordinary resources. Seldom though do we consider their endeavors in light of any particular college curriculum or say to ourselves as we read about them in our local newspapers, "Now that's what a liberal arts education is all about." When these individuals—some with more, others with less on their lists of accomplishments—come to our college doors, we often begin by doubting the relevance of their experientially-gained liberal arts and its application to our classroom expectations. It is as though, in some instances, knowledge and learning are separate from achievement

---

[1] Interested readers might begin by surveying the various articles and bibliographies found in *Enriching the Liberal Arts Through Experiential Learning*, edited by G.E. Brooks and J.E. Althof, Jossey-Bass, 1979.

and living—at the very same time on another part of campus, we may be providing integrated, often expensive, experiential learning opportunities outside the classroom for our more traditionally aged students. This is a curious phenomenon and perhaps one of the most fundamental issues confronting faculty and administrators who seriously want to assess and accredit learning in liberal arts disciplines for students of any age or background.

Faculty and administrators alike need to appreciate that people can and do learn history, literature, science, art, mathematics and the full range of other liberal arts disciplines in the process of pursuing their interests, jobs, political or religious beliefs, etc. For most of us there is little or no separation between living and learning. Our task as assessors and administrators is to help all students—those in our classrooms and those who come with equivalent learning from without—to integrate both their theoretical knowledge and their applied skills to their own individual goals and lives.

What Do We Expect Liberal Arts Students to Know and Be Able to Do?

This question, simple and direct, is often one of the most challenging for liberal arts faculty. Responses may range from, "To be able to pass tests," to "To be able to communicate what they know," to "To develop their research skills," to "To be able to think coherently." When these responses are followed up with "Why?," there is often general laughter or smiling until someone says "That is what students are supposed to do," or "That is what we did as students." The simplicity of the question may belie its importance.

The sad finding is—based on hundreds of conversations with faculty—that many instructors have not considered for many years the essential importance of their academic disciplines, in terms of student attainment. Some faculty members follow syllabi that may have been drawn up before they joined the college or university. And even for the many who develop their own syllabi, the focus is more often than not on providing inputs—conveying information, providing lists of readings, administering tests. It is rare to find a teacher who begins his or her course preparation by asking, "At the end of the term what do I expect my students to know and be able to do?"

There is of course the natural assumption that what is taught will be learned and that those elements are what in fact the student should know. Assumptions and tests reflect faculty inputs, and grades are determined by estimating what a student knows in light of those inputs. Rarely do we consider—much less assess—the full range of theoretical knowledge and applied skills that we hope (intuitively, at least) students will have acquired.

Our question then is how can liberal arts disciplines be analyzed to extract those critical elements we want each student minimally to acquire?

A few approaches may be helpful. As is described in Chapter 1, colleagues from a common department may want to analyze each course or content area by describing the general areas of competence that mark the successful student at various levels. To get started with this exercise the group may want to review and refine the broad objectives or expected achievements of the course or discipline. Under each of these categories, they may then want to derive the more specific areas of expected knowledge and competence. In this process there will be much discussion and debate about the relevance of particular topics, the use of language, etc. Most faculty, though, find the process intellectually stimulating and thought provoking. In essence, each member of the department is being asked to consider what is important about his or her discipline or work. Arriving at consensus about the important elements in a subject area then enables the group to determine those elements of knowledge and capability that should be the expected outcomes for all students. While faculty approaches may vary in teaching or facilitating learning, this method provides a framework for conducting fair and reliable assessment for all students.

This process in more detailed form is known as DACUM, short for Developing a Curriculum, a procedure that is widely used to derive lists of competencies primarily in occupational areas. It has been successfully used, however, in a number of traditional academic settings.[2]

Knowledge and Application:
What Is the Balance?

Faculty discussions that lead to the identification of agreed upon capabilities often lead to questions about the role of knowledge

---

[2] Readers interested in learning about other methods of getting panels of experts to develop lists of agreed upon competencies should also investigate the DELPHI procedure in which faculty experts work independently.

or theory and the application of that knowledge or theory. There are faculty who maintain that it is essential for students to know a set of particular theories ("pure knowledge"); others will argue that there is no such thing as "pure knowledge" and that knowledge without application is a hollow pursuit. This is a particularly relevant matter when it comes to matters of assessment.

It might be argued that there are at least two kinds of knowledge which can and ought to be assessed. The first of these is those things that must be known and understood in order to perform or complete a particular task. The second is that knowledge or understanding that serves to underpin or extend performance or competence but which may not be implicit in performance observed through a single activity or over the short period of time which generally characterizes most forms of assessment. Two examples may serve to distinguish these forms of knowledge.

Take, for example, the notion of organization. In preparing written essays or oral presentations most faculty would agree that students should be able to organize their material appropriately. On the basis of the student's products or performances, the assessor would be able to evaluate the student's knowledge and understanding of both the concept and the application of the notion of organization. In making the evaluation most faculty members would have a clear notion of the purpose of the organization and would be able to evaluate whether the student's work satisfied that purpose. A separate test on organization would be redundant. But what of the power law in electricity [power (watts) = current (amps) x potential difference (volts)]? Would we expect all students who learn this law to be able to determine current demand of electrical equipment? If not, why have them memorize the relationship? Would this knowledge serve as an underpinning to future understanding or enhance competence in other activities or pursuits? Would it be appropriate to have students learn the relationship without intention of application? If so, how do we devise an appropriate test? How do we know we will not be testing for rote memory? Or perhaps we want to test a student's ability to memorize?

It may be helpful to identify the knowledge and understanding required to implement the application of learning. The following categories may be useful (Manpower Services Commission (MSC) Technical Advisory Group, 1987):

facts: data or information, physical or natural "laws," sources of information

terminology:	academic, technical or occupational descriptions or definitions
conventions:	symbol systems, ways of doing things, customs and practices
trends/ sequences:	known inferences, known procedures
principles:	scientific "rules" or "laws" which allow data and information to be manipulated
criteria:	ways of making judgments and evaluations
methods:	ways of doing things, using accepted methodologies
theories:	ways of describing and analyzing data and information that make reliable predictions possible
situations:	ways of describing relationships between things (objects, people, symbols, etc.)

The ownership of knowledge per se, or the acquisition of knowledge for knowledge's sake has often been criticized. The reiteration of facts has been discredited as an indicator of true intellectual ability since it could stem from rote learning, and it rarely, if ever, serves a useful function in life by itself. Knowledge of a sequence of dates for example is of little value as a "stand alone" piece of information. Similarly, even knowledge of terminology without a context may be misleading or useless, except for its own enjoyment. To be of value, knowledge must be understood in some context.

But even here it is not the knowledge alone which serves to indicate a person's intellectual ability. Rather it is a function of the complexity of the context and the range and diversity of knowledge which has to be accessed within the application. In a like manner, when we speak of understanding we generally accept that there are different levels of understanding. The nature of the desired understanding is a reflection of the various applications of that understanding.

For example, in the context of heat transfer, it may be sufficient for the understanding to be limited to knowing the factors which influence the rate of heat transfer under steady state conditions; or, alternatively it may be necessary to address issues pertaining to an unsteady state. Additional variable boundary conditions may also exist. Each of these considerations would effect the scope and level of expected student performance and understanding.

Look at another example: to comment on the status of women in the 15th century an individual might draw on literature, art or music of the period. Would we expect students to have a comprehensive knowledge of all sources in all languages and expressed in all forms of media to complete this assignment? Of course not. We would expect any given student to have a subset of information to draw on; and the perspective of the student would vary considerably depending on whether he or she were responding to the issues from the perspective of a psychologist, a sociologist, a historian, a literary analyst, or a music or art critic. Again the exercise would need to be constrained and defined by the purpose. We would expect a wide variety of responses depending on the knowledge-base of the student and his or her ability to manipulate that knowledge in the context.

Thus, ultimately we are concerned with the application of knowledge and understanding. The ability of the student to apply knowledge and understanding depends on factors other than the ownership of knowledge and understanding per se. From the student's point of view we need to ask whether he or she is able to diagnose correctly the purpose of the application, or whether the challenge is expressed in such a way that a competent student should be able to identify correctly the process of the application as well? Can the student establish links, select the relevant facts, compare, contrast, reject or use knowledge that is relevant? Given the continued growth in the diversity and breadth of knowledge and understanding pertinent to any discipline, are not the cognitive skills associated with accessing knowledge and developing understanding more important than the acquisition of only the most basic or essential knowledge or understanding?

In attempting to define more precisely the knowledge and understanding that should be possessed (and demonstrated) by all students seeking credit, it is of value to examine the purpose of the acquisition as a stepping stone to the definition.

The following analysis has been suggested (MSC Technical Advisory Group, 1987):

Knowledge and understanding may be important in the process of

explaining:	summarizing and arranging information
advising:	gathering information, matching information to available options, and suggesting the most effective alternative
translating:	using different words and/or simplifying concepts

interpreting: analyzing and rearranging information, extracting meaning

extrapolating: gathering known data, applying known principles, and suggesting anticipated developments and implications

and in the global activities of

making decisions: seeking out information, matching information to available options and acting on the most effective alternative, and

solving problems: by noticing irregularities, finding out information, matching information to known characteristics, applying problem solving principles, developing potential solutions, acting on the most effective alternative and evaluating the results.

Such an analysis can assist in the identification of essential knowledge, especially in typical problems of the liberal arts which do not have a single correct solution or conclusion, or in which there are alternative, viable decisions to be made.

It is, of course, possible to combine these perspectives in order to develop flexible and reliable assessment procedures. Consider the following:

In order **to explain** how Freud reflected or deviated from certain values of his era, the student will need to know certain facts about the period, methods of research at the time and be able **to interpret** varied historical observations to reflect his or her arguments.

In order **to decide** how best to set up an experiment in the laboratory, a student will need **to consider** various **methods** and **principles** and be able **to work within acceptable conventions.**

In assessing prior experiential learning, it is essential that faculty try to determine with some specificity their expectations of learning. A recurrent issue among some faculty is the suggestion that the theoretical nature of their disciplines makes it impossible to consider learning in terms of expected outcomes and performance criteria. Learning of all types, however, can be analyzed, described and assessed by following the process just presented. By describing the relevance (the application) of theory and knowledge in clear and unambiguous language, both good quality learning and assessment will be facilitated.

How Do We Know When an Adult Student Meets the Specified Criteria in a Liberal Arts Discipline?

The quick answer to this question is to say that if the learning outcomes and performance criteria are in place, the assessor simply matches what the student claims to know and be able to do with the specific outcomes and performance criteria. But this process is often not as simple as it seems owing to the fact that generally people do not learn in the way in which we arrange our curriculum and frequently they do not have evidence to prove explicitly all we expect of them. This circumstance is particularly common when it comes to assessing adults, who are often rich in applied learning but weaker in theoretical areas. While it is indeed possible to make inferences about a student's knowledge or theoretical understanding on the basis of an evaluation of successful past or current performances or products, there may be instances in which further assessment of knowledge or theory is needed since particular forms of evidence or procedure seldom can encompass or reflect all circumstances in which the theory or knowledge may be required. Faculty will need to determine the nature of acceptable evidence to verify the level of learning as expressed in the learning outcome statements. It may be necessary in these circumstances for the assessor to devise a simulation or actually administer a form of written or oral examination in which the desired knowledge or theory could be expressed or demonstrated in the exceptional ways sought.

To underscore some of these issues, we can consider a few elements from one of the examples given in the beginning of this chapter. With his two published historical novels, John could provide assessors with concrete evidence of his learning achievements in English composition, British and American history and creative writing. In essence the assessors in each of these disciplines would need to see if John's work met the specified learning outcomes and performance criteria within each discipline. They would also want to ensure that the two books were actually the products of John's hand.

For the assessor to assure this achievement, the assessors might give John a set of the learning outcome statements with performance criteria for each and ask him to identify aspects of his writing that met the specified criteria. He might, for example, know a great deal about 18th century England but little about the 20th century.

Depending on what was required by the department, John's evidence as conveyed in his books might or might not be sufficient. If the assessors felt that John's books in of themselves did not indicate an adequate breadth of learning, they might set up an interview in which his learning could be further explored and verified. The evidence in his books might serve as a "road map" to the interview or to further suggested learning.

Similarly, if the outcomes for creative writing at John's institution required that students also demonstrate competence in poetry and the short story and John had never worked in these forms, he might not be eligible for credit in this area or that particular course. John might then more appropriately seek to have his learning assessed or accredited in "The Novel" or in an independent study course in writing.

Keeping in mind that the assessment of prior learning is an attempt to maximize flexibility for both students and assessors while ensuring academic credibility, liberal arts assessors need to draw on their own creative resources to develop sound alternatives for themselves and their students. They need to recognize that learning can be acquired from endless human endeavors and that the application of learning is often the best indicator of mastery of a given theory or knowledge-based discipline.

References

Brooks, G.E. and Althof, J.E. (Eds.). *Enriching the Liberal Arts Through Experiential Learning.* San Francisco: Jossey-Bass, 1979.

Manpower Services Commission (MSC) Technical Advisory Group, Working Document. Crown Copyright, 1987.

Susan Simosko author of Earn College Credit for What You Know, has served CAEL both as a member of the central staff and as a consultant. She recently formed her own business in Sheffield, England and provides training, assessment and evaluative services to organizations in Great Britian, the United States and elsewhere. Her address is 20 Chorley Drive, Sheffield, England Sl0 3RR.

Graham Debling is Head of the Methodological Unit of the Manpower Services Commission, Sheffield, England. The Commission is concerned with the development of competence-based criterion-referenced standards.

Chapter 5
Issues in Assessing Occupational and Technical Subjects

Patricia Dewees

Introduction

During the 1980s, there was a significant increase in the number of individuals requesting prior learning assessment of their skills and knowledge in technical subjects. With the de-industrialization of the American economy, skilled technical workers began to find certain job markets closed and others extremely competitive for the first time in the history of the American labor force. In any tight job market, credentials become important and employers begin to select their employees on the basis of formal credentials such as college degrees. This has been a trend throughout the 1980s. Community and technical colleges have responded by developing curriculum and credentials for many trades which were formerly learned on-the-job during some form of workplace apprenticeship.

Good practice and solid standards for the assessment of prior learning are not dramatically different for technical subjects than for others, but there are a few means of assessment which potential assessors and administrators may wish to consider as ways to facilitate adequate and economical assessment in technical areas. Some examples will introduce these assessment mechanisms.

Licenses

David H. joined an engineering firm as a beginning land surveyor at age 21 after one year of college. He was given extensive on-the-job training, working in over twenty counties under the supervision of a surveyor. He enrolled in an International Correspondence Study (ICS) home study course in mapping and methods of surveying and was also sent by his firm to numerous workshops and seminars. After several years with the firm, David took and passed the two-day State Board Examination for Professional Land Surveyors Registration. Passing this examination allowed him to be responsible for his own surveys. Later he supervised other crew chiefs in the field. David decided to earn an Associate Degree from his local Community College. He was able to earn prior learning assessment credit for Surveying I, II, and III, a total of 9 credits. His primary documentation was his state surveyor's license from the Professional Engineers and Surveyors Board.

In many technical areas, a license speaks to the fact that a recognized body has verified that the licensee has the necessary level of competency. Other licenses with similar acceptance include certain pilots' licenses (F.A.A. Commercial Pilot Certificate), and those for radiologic technician (AART exams), Real Estate Broker, and Certified Quality Control Inspector (ASQC). In some cases, the license is the only documentation required by an evaluator in the assessment process.

The possession of a journeyman's card in the skilled trades is often equal to holding a professional license. The journeyman's card represents a documented record of on-the-job training coupled with a prescribed curriculum of related education. In the last decade, almost all related instruction has been delivered by community and technical colleges. Previously, related instruction may have been available only through adult vocational educational programs (non-credit) or in remote areas, through non-credit correspondence study. However, even this less documented learning, coupled with significant job experience, often has proven to be equal to college level learning.

Direct Credit for Professional Training

Many colleges now grant direct credit for professional technical training which results in a license or journeyman's card. This recognition happens in one of three ways:

1. If the training that resulted in the awarding of professional certification has been evaluated by the American Council on Education (ACE) and appears in the Guide for the Program on Non-Collegiate Sponsored Instruction (PONSI), some col-

leges and universities will place the credit directly on the student's transcript.

2. A college may actually perform its own evaluation of the training following guidelines similar to those developed by ACE. Faculty from the institution review the curriculum, materials, and instructor credentials to determine a credit award for students who complete the program. This process and format has been detailed by the Vermont Office of External Programs, Education and Training Evaluation Service (OEP/ETES) through the support of a FIPSE grant to develop better collaboration between business and industry.

3. A variation of this program evaluation is to require the first few students with professional documentation to undergo a complete assessment process, articulating their learning and providing full documentation. Thereafter, students with identical documentation are awarded credit directly. This process is employed by North Shore Community College of Beverly, Massachusetts, which now offers credit for over 75 licenses and certificates.

Increasingly colleges now deliver part of the education and training needed to complete a license or journeyman's card. One of the earliest joint ventures of this kind was the "dual enrollment" program developed by the National Joint Apprenticeship and Training Committee of the IUOE (International Union of Operating Engineers) which in 1975, had over two thousand apprentices enrolled in college degree programs in approximately twenty locals of the Union. More recently, the Vermont OEP/ETES program found that business and industry were interested in colleges that were able to provide an integrated set of services which began with prior learning assessment of workplace learning and evolved into continuing education delivered by the colleges. The majority of businesses participating in ETES later contracted for further training with Vermont colleges.

Integrating Technical Assessment Credit into the Degree Plan

Paul finished the diesel mechanics training program at the "Roadways" Training School. He was able to use this training to earn an Associate in Technical Studies in Diesel Mechanics at Cuyahoga

Community College. The training was evaluated for credit and Paul finished the general education requirements at the college.

Lately, community and technical colleges have paid more attention to how to incorporate off-campus technical training into the curriculum. Some colleges have developed a generalized Technical Studies degree which uses the student's previous professional training as the area of concentration in the degree. For example, several Ohio colleges offer an Associate in Technical Studies which allows students to earn up to one year's credit for technical training completed off campus. This training may not be already available in the curriculum.

In Dearborn, Michigan, the Henry Ford Community College offers journeymen the chance to use their related education as the first year of an Associate Degree in Science. Journeymen may complete graduation requirements and earn a degree related to their trade such as "Associate in Science, Plant Maintenance Technology."

Rio Salado Community College of Phoenix, Arizona developed a one year intensive competency based Associate in Science Degree, offered at the Motorola Inc. workplace. The degree combined specific job-related skills (microprocessor technician) and the basic education requirements of the associate degree.

Often students intend to change their career by returning to school. Learners may enter a program with prior learning to be assessed in a technical field, but intend to enter a new, non-technical area. If the individual has very little previous college credit, the credit may be used as elective credit. The problem arises when the student has no need of elective credit and also wants to change direction. In those cases, the assessment process is not profitable for the student and should not be undertaken by the college.

Susan M. completed a secretarial training track at the local vocational high school. After graduation, she was employed by the local university as part of the typing pool. After a few years, she joined the university's legal affairs office. She worked there for ten years under the supervision of a senior secretary. When microcomputers were brought into the office, Susan volunteered to become trained. She had an interest and an aptitude for the technology and she designed the database used by the office. She also trained others in the use of different word processing software. Since she had tuition assistance as part of her benefits plan, Susan decided to enter the university to study computer science. She went through the assessment process and earned more than 30 hours of secretarial and office management technology credit which she applied as elective credit in her degree plan.

Articulation Agreements

Individual assessment procedures usually benefit the learner more than articulation agreements with vocational education programs or proprietary schools do. In the case of proprietary schools, the issue of competition confuses the evaluation procedures. Some schools feel reluctant to accept credit in transfer from their competitors.

In fact, as Terrance Dunford of Cuyahoga Community College points out, there is minimal competition between a community college and most trade schools. "Their students choose to forego non-technical education, and as a comprehensive community college, we choose not to offer purely technical programs. To compete for their students we would have to alter our academic structure radically at the cost of losing students to other community and four year colleges. Furthermore, the specialized nature of proprietary and apprenticeship training often precludes the College from competing programmatically." (Dunford, 1987)

Dunford suggests that articulation agreements with proprietary schools can benefit all parties. The proprietary schools offer focussed skills training, intensive training on specialized equipment and often some form of job placement or on-the-job training. The community colleges offer the diagnostic testing, developmental education, and the competencies required for completing the general education requirements of a degree.

Cuyahoga Community College has developed agreements with ten proprietary schools in its region and with four apprenticeship councils. The standards used for the agreements are similar to other accreditation agreements including accreditation by one of the professional technical accreditation agencies like NATS (National Association of Trade and Technical Schools). These agreements are related to the Associate of Technical Studies (ATS) programs.

Vocational schools, monitored by state and national agencies are a different story. As both secondary and post-secondary programs develop competency based curricula, it should become easier to articulate the obvious "ladder" or overlapping programs. The state of Florida has already proposed a common course numbering system for all parts of its state system, high school through university.

For example, a typing course with a particular set of outcomes defined by the state will be numbered "Typing 101" and be worth two credits. The course could exist in a high school, a vocational education program or a college. This arrangement will allow students to transfer credit directly from one program to another.

Budget-minded state legislators are now pushing state funded institutions to collaborate more effectively and to avoid duplication of efforts in training the workforce. Articulation agreements clearly avoid duplication of efforts and facilitate cost-effective partnerships.

On-the-Job Training

Most learners with prior learning in technical fields have had on-the-job training (OJT). In many cases, OJT has been the primary mode of learning.

Gary H. entered the metallurgical industrial labs of his company as an entry level production employee immediately after high school. After several years, he successfully bid on a lab technician position. From this point his talents were recognized by the company and he received extensive company training. Over a number of years he became the Manager of the Metallurgical Laboratories for the company. He completed a diploma in metallurgical technology from the American Society for Metals Engineering Institute and had extensive on-the-job training in complex materials research and quality control projects. He has been extremely active in the professional societies of his trade and has published several articles about processes which he perfected in his work. These organizations also offer continuing education programs in the science of metals.

Gary decided to earn a college degree and, through a portfolio process at a state university, he earned a total of 48 credits. However, most of the credit was awarded in supervision, report writing and other management areas because it was difficult to match his very specific work training to university courses. Gary did earn credit in industrial technology courses in quality control and materials. However, his most technical skills and knowledge are not reflected in his portfolio.

Business and industry currently sponsor enormous and growing training and education enterprises taking place primarily at the workplace. The traditional rationale for training is results oriented; training should bring about increased productivity in the workplace as quickly as possible. Therefore, training is job specific, typically compressed, skill oriented, and competency based. Training is delivered by vendors, by in-house training departments, and contracted out to colleges and to consultants. "Pre-packaged" training programs have increased in popularity and in sophistication. Interactive computer and video disk programs are used extensively in health care and industry.

Workplace training often creates problems in the assessment process. The documentation from training events varies, but can include some or all of the following: certificates of completion, end of course exam grades, time reports, union records, company training department records, and personnel records. These training records alone are seldom sufficient documentation of learning. A few large training departments may computerize training records and be able to offer course materials and more details of the training which could be invaluable during the assessment process.

Occasionally, trainees are sent to a long term program at the national corporate headquarters, a vendor school, or a program at a cooperating college. If the program is of some duration (six weeks, for example) and the course materials are available, then students may reasonably request an evaluation. And, if an individual continues to use the learning acquired in training in his or her job, then the training records along with the evidence of the continued experiential learning on-the-job would be sufficient documentation for the assessment.

Technical learning, like learning in other subject areas, may emerge out of an individual's hobby or interest. Many workers in industry continue part of their work in "moonlighting" and "shade tree mechanics." Some people build or wire their own homes. Another may serve as the chief mechanic for race cars on weekends, operate a ham radio, run a garage welding shop, or demonstrate cabinet making at craft shows. In these examples, some forms of documentation may be difficult or impossible to obtain since the learner is unsupervised.

Demonstration can be one effective form of documentation, and there are some technical skills that are difficult to document short of actual demonstration. If demonstration is used, it is necessary for the integrity of the institution that some form of reporting system is developed and used. The reporting system could be a video tape, an audio tape, or a written checklist. This report becomes part of the student's record in the assessment process.

In some subject areas like metal fabrication or carpentry, a finished product is also excellent documentation that the learner has mastered a set of skills. When a work sample is presented as evidence, the evaluator can effectively interview the learner about the process and the development of the product. If the work sample is large (a garage or house, for example) the instructor may need to make a site visit. Sometimes the evaluator can accept photos if there is sufficient proof that the learner was responsible for the activity.

Testing

Is the learner's knowledge recent or current? This issue becomes particularly important in areas relevant to public health or safety. In addition, the emergence of robotics and computer technology has drastically changed many occupational technical fields. For these reasons, testing may play an important role in the assessment of knowledge in some technical fields.

Vocational education has a tradition of evaluation based on performance testing. Several large testing and curriculum development programs have been in existence for years. One of the largest, VTECS (Vocational Technical Education Consortium of States), based in Atlanta, Georgia, is a project of the Southern Association of Schools and Colleges. VTECS provides a number of services to its members, including comprehensive competency based curriculum materials in many trades. VTECS is developing a computerized validated test item bank based on a skills knowledge analysis of performance objectives. (VTECS, 1985).

NOCTI (National Occupational Testing Institute) designs and administers vocational education certification tests in approximately 50 technical areas. The following section is an example of the nature of the comprehensive testing available through this program:

Airframe and Power Plant

Written Test. General questions on electric circuits in aircraft, weight and balance principles and computation, types of fluid lines and fittings, specifications and requirements for ground operation and servicing, corrosion control, procedures and methods for aircraft inspection; airframe systems and components, including types of structures, principles of operation and methods of servicing; power plant operation and maintenance, systems and components.
Time: 3 hours   No. of Test Items: 183

Performance Test. Hydraulic components and systems, sheet metal work, use of airworthiness directives, engine ignition timing, engine valve service, carburetor service, and generator service.

Time: 5 1/2 hours

The tests are administered nationwide in area test centers. Over 60 colleges and universities grant college credit for these exams, generally in the area of education. NOCTI tests meet state certification requirements in some states. (NOCTI, 1985).

These materials are an excellent resource for college assessors attempting to determine standards for evaluating prior learning in technical subjects.

Portfolios for Technical Courses

The portfolio process emphasizes articulation of learning in written format. It may appear that this mode is less well suited to the technical curriculum. However, a learner can often use a portfolio to demonstrate his or her knowledge of the special language, theory, and practice of a technical subject just as well as in a liberal arts or social science subject area. The following example is from a portfolio petitioning for credit in an upper division course in plastics in the industrial technology curriculum:

> I learned how the heat distortion characteristics of a molded part can vary with molding conditions. Thicker portions of the shot, such as bosses and ribbing, retain greater amounts of heat energy and so cooling lines must be routed nearer these surfaces within the cavity block to prevent distortion and sinking. Cooling water temperature affects the molding process in such a way that there exists an optimum temperature and flow rate which varies with each new mold, and cycle time. Environmental conditions can affect part quality and be compensated with cooling water temperature. Generally speaking, it is better to increase flow rates of cooling water than to decrease cooling water temperature. The reason being internal stresses can be set within a molded part as well as cold flows and inadequate weld joints.

Finally, a reminder about the complex and rich learning experiences of all adult learners. Industrial workers also live a variety of roles and responsibilities, being active in civic organizations, family life, unions, and religious groups. After extensive assessor training and preparation for a group of United Auto Worker/Ford Motor

Company industrial production employees, a few college advisors were surprised to learn that the first successful portfolio submitted for assessment was in philosophy. Or consider this example:

> Michael is a journeyman tool and die maker at Ford. He has always enjoyed helping people and has been active in his union local and in his community. Michael worked as financial secretary for the union local for a number of years. He also trained to be an employee assistance (EAP) counselor. He is currently on the Board of the local credit union.

> Michael applied for credit for the learning he's acquired on his own through the Ohio University Portfolio process. He received credit for the following courses:

> industrial technology .... 15 hours
> accounting technology .... 6 hours
> community health service................................. 15 hours

> These total hours can be applied towards Michael's bachelor's degree.

> The learning required by the tool and die apprenticeship training program is extensive and rigorous. The amount of credit a person receives for prior learning will depend on several factors including where and how an individual completed the related education part of the training and whether or not the college has courses in its curriculum that match the training.

Conclusion

There are many different ways that adults' technical and occupational learning can be assessed. As in all assessments, standards must be established and the most appropriate assessment method explored and used.

Resources

National Occupational Competency Testing Institute
318 Johnson Hall
Ferris State College
Big Rapids, MI 49307

National Institute for Work and Learning
1302 18th Street, NW
Washington, DC 20036

"College Credit for Professional Training: New Challenges to CAEL for the late 80's," Anita Turner in *CAEL News*, May/June, 1987.

VTECS
Vocational Technical Education Consortium of States
Southern Association of Colleges and Schools
795 Peachtree Street, NE
Atlanta, GA 30365

Education and Training Evaluation Services
Vermont State Colleges Office of External Programs
P.O. Box 34
Waterbury, VT 05676-0034

Dunford, Terrence, Cuyohoga Community College. "Articulation of Proprietary Schools and Colleges: A Model." A paper presented at the Seventh National Conference on Adult and External Degree Programs, sponsored by the Alliance and the American Council on Education, Memphis, TN, 1987.

Patricia J. Dewees is a national consultant on adult and experiential learning. She has acted as the CAEL Senior Trainer in designing programs for the assessment of occupational and technical learning. She is Coordinator in the Office of Adult Learning Services at Ohio University.

Chapter 6
Issues in Assessing Business

Michael Mark

Robert is the kind of adult student whom every administrator or instructor likes to use as a case study. In 1965 he began his college career as an education major. His transcript is a demonstration of the "roller coaster" effect some students experience as they go from semester to semester fluctuating between grades of A and F. After a few years of consistently inconsistent performances Robert was married and went to work for an insurance company. Over the next five years he held three different jobs with three different companies and attended college on a part time basis, and his first child was born.

After bouncing around for a few years, Robert found work with a hospital. In 1984, having received a number of promotions and salary increases, he decided to return to college, pursue a degree in business administration, and major in health care management. Upon his return to school he enrolled in an experiential learning program, and through the use of assessment by portfolio he earned 28 hours of credit in various business subjects. By 1985 he had earned a bachelor's degree and had applied for graduate school to pursue an M.B.A.

Mary is yet another excellent case study. She graduated from a non-accredited business school and began her career in 1962 as a secretary to an assistant director. After several odd jobs, she became a clerk in a federal office in 1964 and over the next few years received two promotions within the administrative structure of that bureau. She had described the 1970s as a period in which she was "searching personally" and enrolling in a number of personal growth types of courses for credit and non-credit. She has also described that period of her life professionally as a time of growth. Her promotions have continued through the 1980s.

Through this 25 year period of employment, Mary has partici-pated in numerous workshops, short courses, professional development training sessions, and has earned a total of one year of college credit. Upon her return to college in 1985 she applied for an additional year of credit in areas as diverse as business, political science, interpersonal communications and social work, and received a full year of college credit for the learning demonstrated in her portfolio.

The Faculty Assessors

At Ohio University, where a course match process is used, the faculty who reviewed the portfolios of these students were not unanimous in their decisions to award credit for the various instances of learning presented by the students. Just as there are shining examples of students who exemplify the best qualities of adult students, so too are there faculty members who have accepted the concept of assessing extra-institutional learning and do so with unusual expertise. Below are excerpts of faculty evaluations done for a few of the courses submitted for credit by Robert and Mary.

"I have reviewed your portfolio requesting experiential learning credit for Management 420 (Administration of Personnel). I certainly commend you on the variety of your job experiences and supervisory responsibilities in both insurance and hospital care industries.

"However I do not believe that your experience content actually qualifies you on most of the topics we include in our personnel management course. These include personnel management development stages, personnel department organization, recruiting, selection, induction, training and development, wage and salary administration, fringe benefits development, communications, discipline, personnel research, labor forecasting, and equal employment opportunity.

"Your portfolio suggests considerable reading efforts in most of the areas cited in the previous paragraph. You might want to consider applying for course credit by examination for this course instead of prior learning assessment. Should you decide to exercise this option, I'd be pleased to suggest further reading materials that would help you prepare for this examination."

Another faculty member reviewing Mary's request for credit in Management 430, Management Systems-Decision Making, felt that she met the "basic" course requirements and provided the following assessment of her work:

"Mary's experience is largely on group awareness which is an important aspect of decision making. She also has learned to structure her decision making from problem to implementation. She also uses brainstorming for creativity.

"There is a lack, however, of other aspects of decision making which we now incorporate into Management 430, and she should attempt to provide for those on her own effort:

1) A more conceptual framework of decision making (organizational theory) by levels within an organization;

2) Some exposure to systems theory;

3) Use of computers in the decision making process; i.e. DSS (decision support systems).

The presentation of the student profiles and faculty evaluations is like reading the ending of a good mystery before reading the book itself. The student profiles and faculty comments provide some clarity in analyzing issues in the assessment of business topics. Many of the issues that will be addressed later in this chapter are contained within the profiles and evaluations already presented. It is not a difficult task to cull from the many student files those of students whose lives typify the adult student, nor is it difficult to pull from thousands of portfolio assessments the few that demonstrate a clarity and precision on the part of the faculty that also neatly address many of the assessment issues.

A real concern among practitioners is that there is a high level of expectation on the part of students that assessment credit will be awarded, which expectation is met in part by a conservative faculty reluctant to award credit. Some understanding of this potential conflict is gained by examining the success rates of student portfolios. If there is evidence that students in business have a significantly lower success rate in their portfolio petitions, one might conclude that this potential conflict has manifested itself in the process. The data available from two schools suggests, however, this is not the case.

Hruby (1980) took an in-depth look at the assessment process of Aquinas College and presented a list of course petitions on a department-by-department basis as listed below.

Department	Course Petitions	Success Rate
Business, Accounting	293	69%
Social Sciences	94	73%
Education, Physical Education	81	81%
Science, Engineering	80	85%
Speech, Communications	32	81%

Languages	23	57%
Religious Studies	20	35%
All Others	14	79%

On the surface it does appear that there is some evidence to support the idea that business courses at Aquinas College were the most sought after, and that the success rates of students petitioning those courses were a little lower than the average.

In reviewing the course petitions at Ohio University for a period of 18 months (1986-87) the following departmental listing represents over 80% of the assessments performed.

Subject/Department	Requests	Success Rate
Secretarial Technology	279	81%
Business	180	63%
Physical Education	120	93%
Industrial Technology	72	82%
Interpersonal Communications	68	62%
Aviation Technology	48	100%
Education	37	86%
Electronics Technology	20	75%

Again there is strong surface evidence that might lead to the conclusion that business courses are highly sought after and that business faculty are conservative in their assessments, based on the seemingly low success rate.

Hruby (1980) indicated that the overall high rate of success in petitioning for course credit is due in part to the information students receive early in the program about the various courses and chances of success. After all he writes, "There is little sense in having students do lengthy write ups and petitions for credit in instances where they have little chance for success."

At Ohio University where the assessment of prior learning has been in existence for nearly ten years that type of reasoning is also applicable. Students have the benefits of a portfolio class, many of the courses most sought after will have outlines on file, and there is the opportunity for students to meet with faculty assessors, if appropriate, to discuss their backgrounds and their course selections. Clearly there is ample opportunity and information for the student to make an informed decision and thereby increase the over-all success rate.

But still there is the appearance that high expectation is met with faculty conservatism, and unfortunately there is no good way to measure either. The best that can be offered at this time is obser-vations about both the faculty in business and the students seeking credits in business.

Given the popularity of the business courses, the faculty in the College of Business Administration have gained considerable expe-rience and skill in assessing portfolios. They have made their expec-tations clear, they have re-examined their courses in light of portfolio petitions, and they have come to understand what is acceptable for credit awards. Furthermore, if the faculty were overly conservative, it seems unlikely that so many petitions would come across their desks. What would be a more probable scenario is that the word would get out that they are conservative, and the number of peti-tions would decrease dramatically. So if the observations about fac-ulty are that they are skilled at doing assessments, and are obviously open to the process of assessment, differences must stem from the student side of the formula.

I would suggest that the students who apply for credit in busi-ness courses are more willing to take risks than other students. They are willing to apply for credit in areas in which their backgrounds may not be exceptionally strong, risking failure but in hopes of achieving success.

As the case histories tend to show, those individuals who are seeking credit in business topics tend to be persons who have suc-cessful career tracks. They have moved up in organizations, advanced in their professions, taken on greater responsibilities, and at the same time may have increased their incomes and material posses-sions, all of which are signs of "success." As the reasoning goes, "Business programs educate students to be successful in business . . . I am a success in the business world already . . . therefore I should be receiving business credits." Many program administra-tors can cite instances when this type of reasoning has been used by students before, during, and even after the assessment process has been completed.

Often it is difficult for the successful business person to accept the rationale that the colleges of business are concerned with, and focus on, theory development. Yet, assessors are routinely inter-ested in learning whether the student does have the theoretical base and then whether he or she knows how to apply it. Since the instructors at Ohio University cannot ask the student to demonstrate this knowledge of theory and skill in applying the theory in a paper and pencil test, the adult student must delineate his or her theoretical understanding in the portfolio and must provide documentation which exhibits the application of the theory.

As practitioners are aware, it is the **learning** that is being assessed, not the experience, the portfolio, or the success of the individual. Adhering to this basic principle of good practice should prevent students from taking the shortcut of equating business success with academic success.

Tied to the basic tension between the student and the faculty are the methods each group has used to learn the same or similar sets of skills or theory. The student up until this time has chosen to by-pass the college or university to "earn" his or her success; the faculty member on the other hand has most often used the traditional academic structure to earn his or her rank in the professoriate, which includes much classroom learning and traditional methodologies of demonstrating competencies.

There is little one can do to ameliorate the potential for frustration in which students claim to have learned the same things a faculty member teaches, learned it without benefit of their instruction, and feel that they deserve the same credit as those who sit in the classroom. In the process of assessing students' prior learning, faculty need to view themselves as the expert judges they are and not as teachers. And students must come to understand that academic credits are awarded in terms of competencies or the understanding of a body of theoretical constructs, not by other criteria for success in other pursuits.

How Are Learning Outcomes Determined in the Business Area?

In business courses, and in most disciplines, when a course match process is used, faculty need to develop a set of competency statements and performance criteria to guide their assessments. The competency statements focus on the fundamentals of the course or discipline as evidenced in the evaluation for the Management 420 course. That particular evaluation cited specific areas in which the student did not demonstrate competencies such as selection, induction, salary administration, etc. Often the identified competencies are organized around a textbook that faculty might be using in the course at that time. The awarding of credit, either for classroom learning or portfolio submissions is based on the notion that a student must master that particular set of competencies to earn credit for that course.

To facilitate students' progression through the process, administrators of prior learning assessment programs need to ensure that there is adequate information on hand for the student to gain insight into the required course competencies. At Ohio University an entire file cabinet of course outlines and syllabi is kept along with the learning statements of former students who have sought assessments in various courses. Between the learning statements and the course outlines, the petitioner has an opportunity to review the required competency statements for a course and to make the personal decision as to whether or not to apply for credit for that course.

What About Students Long on Applied Knowledge and Short on Theoretical Knowledge?

The faculty member who did the assessment for Finance indicates that the student's lack of knowledge may be made up with additional reading and a re-submission of the portfolio. The faculty member in Management 420, on the other hand, recommended that if the student who is lacking theoretical knowledge still wants to pursue credits, then he or she may do so by taking an examination. It is also interesting to note that two different methodologies were used in the evaluations done by these faculty members. The finance professor made use of a personal interview in combination with the written portfolio, while the management professor relied only on the evidence submitted in the portfolio.

Regardless of the techniques used in assessments, faculty continue to rely on one common expectation that applies to all students. If the course includes a theory element, students must be able to demonstrate sufficient theoretical knowledge to receive credit for the course. Additional readings and assignments may make up for the lack of theoretical knowledge, or faculty may use another institutional structure to address this issue. At Ohio University any student who lacks theoretical knowledge may do additional readings and sign up for one of hundreds of exam options as was suggested above. Faculty may exercise a variety of options: the student may be required to do a research paper, be interviewed by the faculty member if possible, or complete a special project to make up the lack of theoretical knowledge.

The additional work that faculty may assign or the different assessment techniques they may use are important vehicles for closing the "theoretical knowledge gap" that exists. A second important avenue that is available at Ohio University and other institutions as well is linked to the traditional curriculum. Quite often there are a number of "internship" courses in addition to courses that have been designated as seminar, independent study, or individual reading courses. These courses have been used by the traditional student to make up some of the gaps in practical application that result from not being in the working environment and from accumulating only theoretical knowledge.

For the student with applied knowledge who does not have the theoretical understanding to earn credit in specified courses, he or she may seek credit in one of the "unspecified" courses mentioned above. Those courses might also be used by faculty members who are reviewing specific course petitions and feel that the student has good knowledge, but that the knowledge does not necessarily match the course in which the student is seeking credit. In those instances the faculty member may deny the student credit for Management 420 (Personnel Administration) but may award the student credit in Management 497 (Independent Research) or Management 498 (Internship).

Because students may have some but not all of the skills and knowledge required to earn credit in a specific course, the faculty may use the assessment to enhance the learning process. In assigning students extra work or readings, the faculty role moves beyond that of assessor, and takes a step towards the traditional teaching role. Often it is the blending of the assessment role with the teaching role that insures that the student has both the theoretical and practical understanding necessary to earn college credit.

How Can Assessors Both Uphold Institutional Standards and Be Fair to Students?

Standards for course work and for degrees need to be set by the faculty of the academic department, in this case, business. Usually a business department curriculum review council or some other organized faculty group works on this task. Assessment practitioners always hope that standards and practices set by these councils and committees have all students in mind so that the adult student seeking assessment credits will not have additional hurdles.

A fundamental question revolves around defining the minimal standards acceptable for receiving course credit. Earning credit in a course through the assessment process may mean something different than sitting through the same course in the classroom and receiving credit. Just as no two classroom learning situations are the same, so too the learning experiences of assessment students and classroom students may be quite different. So the real issue for assessors is to determine whether assessment students and 18-year old students sitting in the classroom have the same, or comparable skills and competencies at the time at which they are awarded academic credit for the course. Can the standards be the same, even though different evaluation techniques may be used to make that judgment?

When the prior learning program began at Ohio University, a very select group of students was admitted to the first experimental portfolio development class. They are often referred to as the "superstars" since they needed exceptionally good backgrounds in order to ease faculty fears about awarding credit for prior learning. As the process developed and faculty became more comfortable with their roles as assessors and students were no longer hand picked for the program, the portfolios received were of varying quality. More difficult judgments had to be made since some of the more marginal portfolios had to be considered for credit alongside exemplary portfolios. It was not long before it seemed that portfolio students had to demonstrate their learning at a level that could only be described as exceptional, while the classroom student had the benefit of a grade scale and could receive credit for the same course while doing inferior or "D" level work. Since portfolios were not graded, they had to be exemplary to receive credit; if they were less than exemplary, they were often denied credit.

It would be rewarding to inform the reader that this conflict has long been resolved, but it has not. Efforts are now under way to train faculty more thoroughly to ensure that standards can be comparable regardless of how a student is assessed. In general, faculty are being requested to award credit if students manifest 75% of the listed competencies for a course, instead of demanding they meet 100% of the competencies. Faculty must remember that even a student who knows almost all of the material, may only do an average job of presenting himself or herself. This type of student is sometimes denied credit, when in fact the student may have done the equivalent of "C" work, which should, of course, result in the award of credit.

What Kinds of Evidence or Demonstration Are Acceptable Proof of College Level Learning in Business Areas?

The first type of evidence that a faculty member usually looks for is the clear articulation of theoretical knowledge that closely resembles the body of knowledge necessary to succeed in his or her course. The articulation of that learning is usually the heart of the portfolio. Although the format and the title of that section of the portfolio will vary from institution to institution, it is usually the student-generated learning statements that serve as the first evidence faculty assessors review.

After the learning statements, faculty generally examine the documentation appended to the portfolio. The documentation to support the learning statements will no doubt be as varied as the students in any program of prior learning, and there is no particular set of acceptable support materials. But it is important for faculty to remember that ultimately it is the student's learning that is assessed, not the documents in the portfolio. The documentation or evidence serves as the road map to the student's learning.

Documentation can include third party verifications, examples of the student's work, newspaper clippings, photographs, and other items of evidence that indicate the student did do what he or she claims to have done. In those courses where a theoretical base is required, there is frequently little outside documentation that is used to support the articulation of that knowledge. Instead, the student usually demonstrates through the learning statements a clear understanding of the required theory, makes the connection between theory and application, and then provides evidence of the application within the documentation section. Often students provide bibliographies of books they have read in the field. This record again serves as a basis for further questions by the assessor. By way of example, a student who claims to have knowledge in wage and salary administration may articulate the learning she has acquired in the learning statements, and provide as documentation a set of guidelines she developed that is used within her company. The assessor may need to verify just how much of the document was completed by the student since company manuals and procedures often are the result of more than one person's effort. It is the faculty assessors responsibility to insure that the product claimed by the student really is the result of his or her work.

Although colleges and universities have managed to separate various segments of theoretical knowledge and to package them into units known as courses, the non-academic world does not function in these terms. People seldom learn in the order of our college courses! Consequently it often becomes difficult to find in a single course the content which corresponds to the documented learning claimed by the student. The student who has become a successful manager will no doubt have skills that cut across a variety of courses. To document those course petitions, a student may submit a variety of letters, certificates, newspaper clippings and work samples, each of which individually represents a portion of one or more courses. The assessor must then make an effort to understand the student's working situation, examine the ways in which the student has acquired that learning, and then determine whether or how the documentation fits into this larger picture. The faculty member might decide that an example of the work submitted, although not directly attributable to that student, may be acceptable documentation in light of accompanying materials or a follow-up interview with the student.

How Can Assessors Handle Corporate or Other Non-credit Training or Courses?

This question raises the more fundamental issue as to whether or not there should be a separate method of evaluation for corporate training and courses beyond the options of the portfolio assessment process, subject or course examinations and the American Council on Education's credit recommendations. Is corporate education such that it needs an additional or separate review to determine whether or not such offerings might automatically receive credit?

The arguments for and against this idea are no doubt familiar to many readers. On the one side, it is argued that corporate education is designed specifically for the corporation offering the program, it lacks much of the general theory taught in college classrooms, is taught away from the classroom, and is taught by individuals who are not necessarily "acceptably credentialled" for resident faculty. The other side of the argument suggests that if the corporate class-

room provides all of the basic content of a course, and if the institution accepts the notion of assessment by portfolio or ACE
recommendations, there should be sufficient precedent to develop
yet another form of assessment of the learning outcomes of corporate methodology.

An offer of compromise would be to examine the institution,
study its role and purpose, and explore the possibilities in working
with, instead of against, corporate sponsors of education. For
instance, what would happen if a major industrial corporation
approached College X, stating that it would like its plant employees
(who lacked a college education) to attend the institution and take
advantage of the lucrative corporate or union educational benefits
available to them. Additionally, suppose the corporation required
certain "conditions" or "agreements" from the institution to insure
that both employees and College X benefitted from the cooperative
agreement.

If this contact were to occur, would it be advisable for each and
every student to go through the assessment process, or take an
examination, if they had all been through roughly the same training
and educational programs? If the corporate program has built-in
assessments and recorded results for each individual, the means for
evaluation are present. If the benefit to the institution is sufficient,
then it would seem that the institution's business faculty could be
encouraged to evaluate the training and education programs to
determine which ones might equate to the institutional course offerings. Faculty need to determine whether licenses, apprenticeships,
certificates, etc. unique to the corporation or industry itself would
also warrant the awarding of credit. Again the presence of performance assessments, duly recorded, for each learner would facilitate
a less burdensome review by the faculty.

The issue is not "how" to assess corporate training since there
are many ways to do so, and creative faculty will come up with more,
but whether such assessment should occur. Such an issue is clearly
one for the faculty to determine **as a group**. It is not something that
should be left to the discretion of a single assessor, since the question
involves larger issues. Should the institution decide not to accept
such corporate education in a prescribed format, then what options
are open to the students?

Assessment by portfolio could probably be the best alternative
for students who have undergone corporate or industrial training.
They can be given the opportunity to explain what they have done,

what they have learned, and provide documentation to demonstrate their accomplishments.

How Much Credit Should a Business Student Be Awarded If He or She Is Majoring in Business?

The issue of "how much" credit often stirs deep emotions rather than logical thought. It raises such notions as "We can't give them too much of the degree or it won't mean anything", or "They have to take something from us or it's not our degree", or "They can't get credit for that without first . . . ". What generally happens is that faculty through argumentation, debate, and politics come to some arbitrary number of credits a student may earn towards his or her degree through the assessment process. They may then set a limit on the number of hours a student may earn that can apply to the major. In other words, "It's okay for him or her to earn credit this way, but just don't let those apply to our major".

In limiting students to a set number of hours, most faculty do not realize that it is rare, very rare, for one student to have a background that includes Managerial Accounting, Financial Planning, Economic Theory, Marketing, Statistical Methods, as well as liberal arts subjects. It is unusual and extremely difficult for any student to earn "a whole degree through assessment," particularly at an institution that uses a course match process in its assessments. It is important for faculty and administrators to remember that **ultimately faculty are making exactly the same kind of academic judgments for all students regardless of the assessment methods employed**. It is ironic that the notion of transfer credit is seldom questioned, although the accepting institution usually can not and does not make any academic judgments prior to placing transfer credits on its own transcript. In awarding credit through the assessment process, however, faculty—as in their role as instructors—are the academic quality control for their own institutions.

Conclusion

Business administration is an area that encompasses a wide variety of theoretical and practical courses, and the opportunities for assessing individuals' learning and granting credit for that learning do exist. Done thoughtfully and against pre-determined standards the assessment process can be and is an academically sound method of making academic judgments about students.

Although there are many decisions facing a business department when it begins such a program, there is little doubt that adult students are significantly helped and motivated by this provision to complete their degrees.

In a sentence, business courses can be assessed for credit, and should be assessed in accordance with principles of good practice.

References

Hruby, Norbert J. "The Faculty as Key to Quality Assurance—Fact and Mystique." *Defining and Assuring Quality in Experiential Learning*. Jossey-Bass, Inc., 1980.

Michael Mark is the Director of Adult Learning Services at Ohio University in Athens, Ohio. He has authored numerous articles on the assessment of prior non-sponsored learning and has taught the portfolio development course several times at Ohio University. He is the immediate past president of "The Alliance; an association of alternative degree programs for adults". Also he is the former Vice President of the Ohio Continuing Higher Education Association (OCHEA).

Chapter 7

Issues in Assessing the Performing Arts

Ann Bielawski and Margaret Dunn

Many adults return to, or for the first time enter college with considerable skills and knowledge in one or more of the performing arts. These students develop their competencies through participation in local orchestras, theatres and dance companies. Some have continued childhood studies into adulthood. Others are professionals. The main source of their livelihood is derived from giving regular performances or lessons in a performing art.

Performing arts students come seeking credit in a wide variety of fields and courses:

- Students who are members of professional dance companies might apply for assessment in ballet, modern dance, jazz, or choreography, hoping to earn degrees that will enable them to teach in a college or university once their performing days are over.

- Students who have directed a variety of plays in community theatre might apply for credits in staging and directing to acquire free elective credits towards a degree unrelated to the performing arts.

- Students who are avid fans of the ballet and attend professional performances on a regular basis might seek credit in the history of the dance or dance appreciation.

These are just a few of the kinds of adult learners who come forward to have their performing arts learning assessed for college credit. In every instance faculty assessors need to be able to make judgments about the abilities and achievements of these students and to relate their competencies to the academic curricula of their own institutions.

Issues

While this principle seems clear enough, a number of issues seem to complicate the matter.

For example, the assumption is often made that the performance levels of professional musicians, actors, or dancers are superior to those which might be expected of college- or university-trained students in one of these areas. On both sides of the issue strong arguments often ensue about which mode of learning is more rigorous: "professional training" or "academic schooling."

This issue frequently creates an unfortunate tension between the various providing communities and this, in turn, only serves to confuse significant assessment issues. Who is to determine who is an abler musician; for example, a working jazz musician who has played around the globe for a number of years or a conservatory-trained musician who has chosen to limit his or her performances in order to focus efforts on teaching others? As silly as the argument may appear on paper, it is a very real issue that can provoke heated and often destructive arguments that lead away from the fundamental one of assessing performing arts achievement.

Another significant issue is the one of the currency of the learning claimed. If a person worked as a professional dancer ten years ago, for example, can his or her learning be assessed and accredited? If so, how can the student best prove his or her competence? If the learning should not be assessed for credit, why not?

How best can students in the performing arts document their learning? Must everyone be assessed by performance? How might an assessor have evaluated the skills and knowledge of Jacqueline DuPre, for example, one of the century's acknowledged great cello players, tragically struck down with multiple sclerosis early in her career but still able to teach until shortly before her death in 1987? And what about all those others who never reach fame or fortune through their art but at some time in the past did achieve recognized competence in a given performing art? Can their learning be assessed? Should their learning be assessed? And if either answer is positive, how best should the assessment be carried out.

Learning Outcomes and Performance Criteria

As in all other fields, many of these issues are immediately tempered when learning outcomes and performance criteria are established. If students are to be awarded college credit, then they must be expected to meet the established criteria. Whether they be famous and rich or unknown and simply diligent, the same performance criteria must hold in any assessment of adults' prior learning in the performing arts.

What seems to complicate this matter, perhaps more than in any other field, is that students seldom learn in exactly the way in which they receive instruction. As dancers, musicians, or actors, they do seem to learn—certainly from the students' point of view and often from the teachers'—more holistically with much more learning acquired by experimentation and individual initiative than by a given instructor's curriculum. This phenomenon serves to highlight a number of important elements that require faculty assessors to plan very carefully prior to beginning the assessment process for performing arts students.

By their very nature, the performing arts are meant to be observed and in traditional classrooms, students are observed over the course of a semester. Faculty have the opportunity to consider the students' growth and development in light of the specific outcomes they have set for each particular class (stated or intuitive) or by comparing one student's performance with that of all the others in the classroom. No such opportunity is generally available to the assessor of prior learning, who instead will have only a sample of the student's work to consider, often only one or two performances. Samples of performance may be shown on tape or observed under simulated circumstances. The student may also produce a range of documents or indirect evidence presented in the form of a portfolio for the assessor to consider. How then does the assessor evaluate the work?

Most often good assessors of the performing arts develop checklists reflecting the range of expected achievements in a field, considering both the depth and breadth of the expected learning. As in other disciplines, performance criteria need to be established as well. In other words, the assessors need to determine not only what the students are expected to be able to do but also the standard at which they should be able to do it.

In doing this necessary exercise, faculty will quickly see the progression of learning that may or may not take place in non-classroom achievement but will, in any event, now be able to match students' learning against these outcomes and criteria. If course equivalency recommendations are required by the prior learning assessment system of the awarding institutions, then it will be necessary for the assessor to cluster these outcomes and criteria in light of particular classroom expectations.

A number of different questions arise, however, even when learning outcomes and performance criteria have been established. For example, let us assume that a dancer, aged 30, was a principle dancer with American Ballet Theatre (ABT) before a serious injury one year ago, putting an end to what had been a most successful professional career. She now wishes to obtain a degree in order to obtain teacher certification in physical education with a dance specialization. Her injury, while preventing her from meeting the rigors of professional dancing, does not limit her for normal physical activity, including dance instruction.

She comes to University X with a vast assortment of playbills, newspaper clippings, letters of praise from some of the top dancers and directors in the field, and a Public Broadcasting tape of ABT performing Swan Lake in which she had a major role. How should such learning be assessed and how much credit should she be awarded?

Is there any doubt that she should be awarded credit for her prior learning? If not, should she be given credit for all the introductory level work or only for the upper-level courses that best reflect her final achievements? Is her level of immediate past performance so in excess of what is required of traditional dance students that she should automatically receive the maximum number of credits allowed? Is it necessary to consider her degree and career goals in making the evaluations of her work?

These are some of the critical questions that frequently must be considered on a regular basis by performing arts departments wanting to recognize adults' past achievement for credit. If the learning outcome statements and performance criteria are in place, such an evaluation becomes a relatively simple matter. In this particular example, the student has ample evidence of her skills and knowledge, both direct and indirect; the quality of her professional company and directors is well known, and her career and educational goals are compatible with her past attainments. Most dance faculty would have little difficulty making suitable credit recommendations based on this woman's experiential learning.

But look at another example. John A. had loved music all his life. As a young boy he had studied the piano with a local teacher, sung in the church choir, and in high school had a lead role in the senior musical. Throughout his adult life, he had continued to play popular music at the parties of his friends and sing in the church choir. Having started college but never finished, at age 40 he now wishes to complete his degree in business studies. In the process he would like to have his prior learning in music assessed in order to fulfill some of his free elective requirements. He therefore seeks credit in Basic Piano Techniques, Vocal Music I, and American Popular Music Since the Twenties. How should the assessors proceed? What evidence is there that John has applicable and equivalent learning to those completing the actual college courses in these areas? Where does the assessor begin?

Again, if the learning outcomes and performance criteria are in place, the task becomes more manageable. In this instance, John would have to document either with physical evidence or live performance that he really did have the skills and knowledge he claimed. Unlike the woman in the first example, neither the standards of his teacher or his church choir are known. Further, based on his self-reported ability to play the piano, there is no current physical evidence of the student's depth or breadth of learning. In this instance, more than likely the student will need to give live performances of his skill and knowledge for each course for which he is seeking credit. Beginning with his claim for credit in Basic Piano Techniques, John might be asked to play selected major and minor scales, prepare a selection of specified pieces and sight read a piece at a level appropriate for this course. Again, the exact requirements for the assessment need to be set against the expected learning outcomes and performance criteria for that particular course.

Some readers may wonder about the usefulness in this instance of a letter from John's childhood piano teacher. Could such a letter be used to validate John's learning? In most instances the answer would be "no" since in all likelihood the teacher would not be able to recall with detail the level of John's ability and, even more important, would not be able to attest to John's current ability at the piano.

This last point, the issue of currency, is an important one that must be addressed early on in establishing the performance criteria. If a student can prove without a reasonable doubt that he or she played the piano, for example, at a professional level ten years ago, but for reasons of health or economics no longer does so, should credit be awarded for the learning? Can there be a retrospective assessment for college credit of the individual's achievement? Each college or faculty department will need to decide the answer for itself. However, it is often helpful to remember that academic credits earned ten years ago or more frequently can be applied to current degree requirements. In addition, often such credits can be transferred to a second institution. No attempt is usually made to verify the currency of the student's learning in a particular discipline or authenticate the standards or assessment methods applied at the previous institution for that course. One might argue on this basis, then, that if students can demonstrate beyond a reasonable doubt that the learning acquired ten years ago satisfies a current institution's requirements in a particular discipline or course, then credit should be awarded.

On the other hand an assumption is often made that the awarding of credit reflects the standards set for academic performance by a given institution. It is generally assumed that credits awarded indicate that a student possesses skills and knowledge in keeping with these academic standards and that a student earning such credit will be able to do something reflecting those standards of achievement. But suppose that last year, College B awarded six credit hours in ballet to a student who over the summer was tragically struck down in a car accident. The student is now confined to a wheel chair. Would the college retract those six credit hours? Hardly. Academic credit awarded and transcripted is not retractable regardless of how much or how little a graduate of that course or institution forgets or is unable to do at a later point. These questions serve only to underscore the complexity of the issues at hand.

For the other courses for which John is seeking credit, he would probably need to undergo an in-person performance assessment. Although he may have sung in the church choir for 25 years, the assessor(s) will need to know that he meets the full range of learning outcomes and performance criteria for Vocal Music I. Very often adult students have a great deal of learning in one particular aspect of a discipline, but fail to have the full range of equivalent learning that could be considered comparable to someone's completing the actual curriculum in that course or set of courses.

To earn credit for his knowledge of American Popular Music, an assessor might set up an oral interview with John, ask him to take a paper and pencil test, prepare an annotated discography, or do a combination of all three.

These two examples serve to illustrate some of the challenging questions that face assessors in the performing arts. Issues of past performance level and experience, the appropriateness of the evidence, and the currency of both the learning and the evidence all need to be addressed as an integral part of the assessment process. The establishment of learning outcomes and performance criteria will help to make the decision-making process easier and more reliable, but individual differences will continue to challenge faculties' creative techniques for assessing the learning and for providing fair and reliable judgments over time.

L. Ann Bielawski is Director of Prior Learning Assessment at Thomas A. Edison State College of New Jersey. She is currently working on her Doctorate in Counseling Psychology at Rutgers, The State University of New Jersey.

Margaret Dunn is Professor of Communications and Theater at Kean College, where she has also directed a number of plays and is the Coordinator of the Core Course Program. She is Co-director for the Center for Global Studies. At Edison State College she sat on the Academic Council and continues to evaluate portfolios. She has conducted workshops and authored numerous articles in the field of Oral Interpretation and Readers Theater.

Chapter 8
Assessment of Professionals
Donna S. Queeney

In discussing assessment of professionals, it is important to define the term "professional," for it is an elusive word used differently in different contexts. In this chapter, "professionals" will be defined as those individuals engaged in practice within a field that has its own body of knowledge and for which specialized education or training is required. Although this broad definition does not specify a level of education required to attain professional status, the author's experience in working with professions and occupations indicates that an individual generally considers what he or she does to be professional in nature, while what the other person engages in is considered an occupation. Thus, to avoid matters of controversy and offense, the broader definition is chosen. This definition also makes sense for this particular discussion because the concepts to be considered can be applied equally well across a large number of professional and occupational fields.

Professionals might be assessed for many different reasons. Frequently employers use formal assessment to identify individuals suited for promotion or advancement. Conversely, assessment frequently is used to identify weak employees so that appropriate remedial action can be taken. Professionals can also be assessed as a means of measuring the health, or quality, of practice within a profession. This chapter, however focuses on assessment of professionals to identify areas of weakness within their practice patterns that might be amenable to correction through educational programming.

It should be noted that the same assessment exercises used to identify areas of weakness within professional practice also can be employed to define areas of strength where no further education or intervention is necessary. Particularly for those professions requiring continuing professional education for relicensure, this is a critical point: can professionals reasonably be required to attend educational programs addressing topic areas in which they have demonstrated competence? The issue of mandatory continuing professional education is a controversial one which is too complex to address here. Yet one must acknowledge that if the purpose of mandatory continuing professional education is to maintain and improve practitioners' competence, and if some practitioners have demonstrated competence in a given area, their need for the particular educational experience is doubtful.

The Need for Assessment of Professionals

Continuing professional education—education to help practicing professionals remain competent within their fields—has been the object of considerable attention for some years. The increasing pressure for recurrent education has been the result of a steadily rising concern with professional competence. When the growth of knowledge and the pace of change were relatively slower, practicing professionals were able to maintain a reasonable level of professional competence based on their initial education and training. However, beginning in the 1960s, a number of new developments, most importantly the expansion of knowledge in science and technology, rendered preprofessional education inadequate to sustain a competent level of practice throughout a professional's career.

At the same time, public accountability for professional competence increased. As Cyril O. Houle (1980) observed in his seminal book on continuing professional education, the needs of society demanded improvement in professional practice, which in turn required improved lifelong learning. Professional practitioners were accused of not remaining competent (assuming that they were competent in the first place) or of not keeping up with current information in their fields. Sometimes they were faulted for not being stimulated by interaction with peers in a learning environment, or for not receiving any feedback on whether or not they were doing well or even passably. Newly trained practitioners across the professions were being set out on the streets with only their preprofessional education and essentially being told that they were set to practice for life. Earn a degree in architecture, pass the registration examination, and you need never learn another thing.

The issue of the merits (real or imagined) of continuing professional education has grown in importance and intensity over the last decade. Continuing professional education initially was grasped at by many in an attempt to stem the tide of criticism, to find a panacea for the ills threatening the health of professions. It seemed so easy, so neat a solution. Professional competence is in doubt? Remedy with continuing education.

However, the public is not easily fooled, and thus it was not long before those concerned with the broad issue of improving professional practice sent up the cry that, indeed, the emperor had no clothes. Abundant continuing professional education could be offered, even required, **but until a link was established between continuing professional education participation and improved practice, nothing would be accomplished in the fight for professional competence.**

Conscientious professionals have long recognized the potential value of continued learning in maintaining their competency, but their selection of learning experiences has been haphazard at best. As opportunities for continuing professional education expanded in response to growing concerns with competency maintenance, the resultant range of choices further complicated the issue. Practitioners were confronted with a vast array of possible learning experiences and little guidance regarding the making of an intelligent selection. Is it reasonable to expect that a midcareer practitioner, expert in his or her profession, also has the expertise required to identify his or her practice-related educational needs and to select educational opportunities to address those needs? It is true that in some cases learning needs are obvious: the tax accountant, for example, must learn about new tax laws. In many instances, however, the need for learning is not so apparent. The practitioner's greatest educational need may be related to tasks performed routinely in daily practice over a number of years. Thus the same tax accountant who recognizes the need for information on new tax laws may not be adequately eliciting information from clients, and may have an unrecognized educational need for communications and interviewing skills.

If continuing professional education is to improve practitioners' competence, it must address their practice-oriented needs. This realization requires identification of those needs, which in turn implies assessment of professional practitioners' strengths and weaknesses in performing the tasks that comprise their daily practice.

Assessment of professional practice requires examination of more than knowledge alone. While professionals certainly must possess a core of knowledge relevant to their field, it is the application of that knowledge in the practice setting, or the demonstration of skills, that distinguishes the competent practitioner from one who is less than competent. Thus assessment of skills, the integration of knowledge into patterns of practice, is essential to measurement of competency (or a lack thereof), and hence to identification of educational needs. It is these educational needs that must be addressed through continuing professional education programs if such programs are to have an impact on professional competence.

Assessment of professional practitioners, with identification of their learning needs and prescription of appropriate educational programming, speaks for itself and is easily understood. Yet group assessment merits consideration. Leaders within a number of professions have indicated that their practitioners share certain weaknesses. Communications skills, adherence to legal guidelines, and ability to integrate various aspects of patient care, for example, are "generic" weaknesses that have been identified in given professions. In cases such as these, assessment of a representative sample of practitioners can and does uncover areas in which the profession as a whole needs further education.

One Approach: The Practice Audit Model

Research conducted in the late 1970s with pharmacists at The Pennsylvania State University resulted in the development of a model for assessment of professional practitioners' educational needs and design of programs to address those needs (Smutz et al, 1981). This seven-phase Practice Audit Model (Figure 1) is based on collaboration of higher education and the professions to develop and deliver optimum continuing professional education. Collaboration is accomplished through the work of a profession team for each field under consideration, the team consisting of representatives of (1) the appropriate academic discipline, (2) state and national professional associations, and, where applicable, (3) the national regulatory agency. The work of each profession team is guided by the model and facilitated by a continuing professional education staff member.

Identification of Areas for Needs Assessment

Underlying the model is the assumption that in order to assess practitioners' abilities to perform the tasks that comprise their

Figure 1
Practice Audit Model

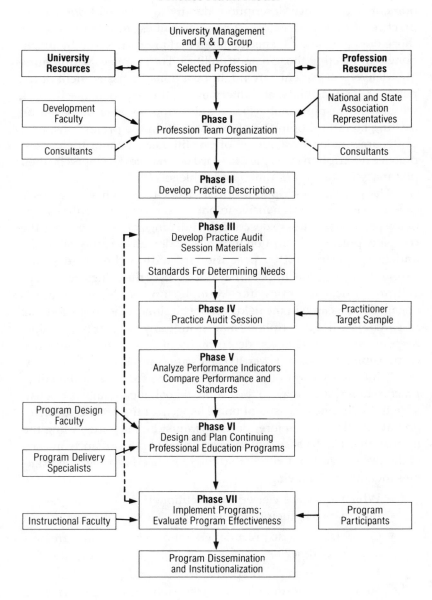

professional practice, it is first necessary to identify those tasks. Thus the Practice Audit Model suggests that the initial step in assessing needs of practitioners of a specific profession is the development of a practice description identifying (1) broad domains of practice of that profession, (2) responsibilities included in each of those domains, and (3) specific tasks that are carried out by practitioners in meeting those responsibilities. For example, within nursing, delivery of patient care might be a domain, assessment of the patient a responsibility, and interviewing the patient a specific task within that responsibility. Practice descriptions may be based on existing literature, opinions of experts within the professions, and/or documentation by a survey of practitioners. One of the earliest practice descriptions was the **Standard of Practice** developed by their pharmacy profession (Kalman and Schlegel, 1979).

The practice description, or role delineation as it sometimes is called, must be comprehensive in nature and cover the entire scope of the profession if it is to describe the full range of practice. Thus the complete practice description includes all domains, responsibilities, and tasks performed by practitioners within the professions, although any one practitioner may not do all of the things described. Within clinical dietetics, for example, one finds practitioners engaged in research in the field, yet not all clinical dietitians conduct research. Practice descriptions may include any number of domains, responsibilities, and tasks; descriptions of from ten to thirty-five responsibilities and well over 100 tasks are common.

While assessment of practitioners on the contents of the entire practice description may be the eventual goal, it generally is not feasible to undertake assessment on all aspects of the practice description at one time. Therefore, decisions must be made regarding the priority that will be assigned to assessment of performance on each of the tasks included. Criteria that might be used in assigning priorities include the following:

- Which areas are viewed by practitioners as being of greatest importance to their practice?
- On which tasks do practitioners report spending the greatest amount of time?
- In which areas do "experts" in the field (e.g. employers, supervisors, leaders in the profession) believe practitioners may be weak?

- In which areas would weaknesses, if identified, be amenable to correction by educational programming?

It should be noted that if an assessment of professional practice were being conducted for other than educational purposes, at least some of the criteria might be different.

Conducting the Needs Assessment

In the early 1980s Penn State, the W.K. Kellogg Foundation, and fourteen participating state and national professional associations joined in support of the five-year Continuing Professional Education Development Project. Guided by the Practice Audit Model, this project assessed practice-oriented needs of practitioners in five professions—accounting, architecture, clinical dietetics, clinical psychology, and nursing—and developed and delivered continuing professional education programs to address those needs. In assessing needs, the goal was to identify needs of the total body of practitioners within a profession rather than the needs of individual practitioners. Thus sample groups of practitioners were selected to represent the profession. The same assessment exercises could be used for individualized assessment, but would be extremely costly when applied on a per person basis.

Assessment center methods were used to assess for all five professions. Samples of approximately forty-eight Pennsylvania practitioners were selected for each profession and invited to participate in a day-long Practice Audit Session. In addition to focusing on measuring practitioner skills, project personnel strove to put as much variety as possible into each of the sessions and to establish an atmosphere in which those being assessed would feel comfortable. Emphasis was placed on the notion that because the goal was development of continuing professional education programs for groups of practitioners, interest was in performance of the group, not of individual practitioners; thus no one felt threatened. To further enhance the climate, practitioners were divided into small groups of from four to six persons, each led by a member of the profession team. This step enabled establishment of an atmosphere of collegiality which made the subjects feel comfortable and ready to concentrate on the tasks at hand without feeling self-conscious.

The assessment exercises developed for the five professions varied greatly. Each exercise was developed by the appropriate profession team—University faculty members, representatives of state and national professional associations and regulatory agencies, and project staff members—working in conjunction with consultants and others in the organizations represented in the project as deemed appropriate. The goal of the exercise was, of course, to assess certain practice-related skills of the practitioners. Some examples of the exercises follow.

- The Nursing Profession Team developed a videotape with which to assess practitioners' abilities to discern appropriate and inappropriate nurse behaviors in dealing with a physician, a dying patient, and the patient's family. The script for the videotape was outlined by the entire Nursing Profession Team, written by one team member, then reviewed by the team and by a consultant. Professional actors and actresses from the community were used and the videotape was produced by Penn State's Division of Learning and Telecommunications Services. The production of the tape represented a real collaborative effort in its own right.

- Both the Clinical Dietetics and Nursing Profession Teams developed live simulations to assess practitioners' abilities to interact with, assess, and teach patients. Both groups happened to write a diabetic patient into their scripts. The actresses trained to portray these patients found this assignment to be a new experience for them. Rather than acting to entertain, or improvising according to cues from the assessees, they had to learn to maintain a consistent posture through twenty-four different nurses or dieticians. One reported that she was happy to go home and raid the refrigerator after hearing about diabetic diets all day.

- Another live simulation was for accounting and featured a company president who barked at each of the accounting practitioners sent in to "work" with him, "My name is Black and I've never been in the red." This exercise was designed to measure participants' skills in interacting with clients.

- The accountants also had made some paper and pencil exercises, dealing with tax preparation and audits. In these, as in a number of other exercises, appropriate forms, charts, and other papers taken from actual practice settings were given to the assessees as they began to work.

- Clinical psychologists participating in that group's practice audit session had to deal with a "depressed patient"—twice.

This was the only profession that included a follow-up interview in the day's activities. An interesting sidenote to this exercise is the fact that one of the actors portraying the depressed patient actually found himself in a fairly depressed state once the sessions were over.

- The entire Architecture Practice Audit Session was based on a single case study, one built around the design and construction of a town hall for the fictitious community of Bald Knob. While most, if not all, of the professions included at least one case study, only the architects carried it to this extent, using it to measure a variety of skills ranging from construction observation and project scheduling to cost control.

Evaluating the Results

As each exercise was developed, plans were made to evaluate the results. For every exercise, for each of the five professions, the profession teams devised detailed rating scales and/or guidelines and forms.

A number of live simulations were used, as noted. These were videotaped for later rating. (At one time consideration was given to evaluating the simulations through one-way mirrors as they took place, but it was determined that this was not a good alternative. Because the simulation would not be recorded, evaluation would have to be completed on the spot, with no opportunity for reconsideration or for review of areas about which raters disagreed.) For those live simulations in which interpersonal skills were being assessed, interdisciplinary teams of raters were used, with one rater from the professional area in which the assessment exercise was being conducted (e.g., dietetics, accounting) and one from the counseling area. In all cases, more than one rater was used.

For all exercises, including the live simulations, rater training was extensive. A consultant was hired for this purpose. After an initial training period, raters scored pilot tests of the particular exercise on which they were working, and shared and discussed their ratings of these items with members of the appropriate profession team. With this careful training, inter-rater reliability was quite high.

Value of the Assessment

Data gained from the assessment exercises permitted identification of areas of practice in which professionals demonstrated weaknesses, indicating educational needs. For example, it was found that nurses are weak in the preparation of nursing care plans, and clinical dietitians have difficulty integrating the various components of their work into a coherent plan. Cost estimating gives architects a hard time, and clinical psychologists do not consider the legal ramifications of their work as they should.

A further benefit of the Practice Audit Sessions in which the assessment exercises were conducted was that the practitioners who participated in them felt that they learned from the experience. Although the exercises were designed to collect data, the professionals viewed them as a valuable learning experience. They identified some of their own weaknesses as they worked, and because of the small group format, they benefitted from interaction with their peers.

A number of continuing professional education programs were developed on the basis of data collected at the five Practice Audit Sessions. As these programs were developed, the relationship of the material being presented to daily practice was a key concern. The design and delivery of such practice-oriented programs is costly. Often videotaping, individual simulations, and other methods must be employed if the program is to meet its goals. Such programs are labor-intensive, with the staff:participant ratio quite high. However, participant evaluations regarding the quality of the programs and their applicability to improving practice indicate that the product may well be worth the expense.

Conclusion

Traditionally, providers of continuing professional education have used one of several methods illustrated on the continuum below to select topics for their programs.

Instructor wants to offer it	Program sells well	Topic is "hot" or fashionable	Practitioners have said they would like it	Employers or supervisors have said they feel there is a need

As can be seen, the relationship between the reason for offering the program and professional practice increases as one moves along the continuum from left to right, but the closest one comes to the reality of practice is relying on informal observations and perceptions. Assessment of professionals' performance is well off the continuum, for it clearly ties topic selection to practitioner skill and thus can provide the link between competence and practice which the public and the professions seek. For the cycle to be complete, however, further assessment is required, and that is an assessment of professionals' performance following participation in the educational programs designed to meet identified needs.

These procedures, and the programs that may be designed as a result of the data they produce, are costly and cumbersome. For this reason, acceptance has been slow. However, for those professions concerned with competency of their practitioners, and for those fields with which the consuming public has a real concern, they appear to be the best, if not the only, answer.

Suggested Activities

1. Name ten types of professionals (using the definition of "professional" stated at the start of this chapter) with whom you come into contact fairly frequently. Consider how important you consider the competence of each to be to your physical, mental, and financial well being, and list them in descending order according to that importance. Next consider the ease of difficulty of assessing the performance of each, and list in descending order of ease. Compare the two lists.

2. With one or more colleagues, identify five key tasks frequently performed by persons in your field. Discuss methodologies that could be used to assess performance of those tasks, considering the strengths and drawbacks of each methodology.

3. Consider the task that is an integral part of your daily work. Develop an exercise to assess your performance of that task, including identification of criteria indicating satisfactory performance.

References

Cervero, Ronald M. "Continuing Professional Education and Behavioral Change: A Model for Research and Evaluation," *The Journal of Continuing Education in Nursing*, Vol. 16, No. 3 (May/June 1985): pp. 85-88.

Cervero, Ronald M. et al, ed. *Problems and Prospects in Continuing Professional Education* (New Directions for Continuing Education). San Francisco: Jossey-Bass, 1985.

Chernoff, Ronni et al, "Continuing Education Needs Assessment and Program Development: An Alternative Approach," *Journal of the American Dietetic Association*, Vol. 83, No. 6 (December, 1983): pp. 654-660.

Crowe, Mary Beth et al. "Delineation of the Roles of Clinical Psychology: A Survey of Practice in Pennsylvania," *Professional Psychology: Research and Practice*, Vol. 16, No. 1, (1985): pp 124-137.

Gross, Stanley J. *Of Foxes and Hen Houses*. Westport, Connecticut: Quorum Books, 1984: Chapter 7.

Henretta, Carol B. et al. "A Needs Assessment in Continuing Professional Education," *Mobius*, Vol. 4, No. 2 (April, 1984): pp. 34-48.

Houle, Cyril O. *Continuing Learning in the Professions*. San Francisco: Jossey-Bass, 1980.

Kalman, Samuel H. and Schlegal, John F. "Standards of Practice for the Profession of Pharmacy,: *American Pharmacy*, March 1979: pp. 21-35.

Lindsay, Carl A. et al. "Continuing Professional Education for Clinical Psychology: A Practice-Oriented Model," *Evaluation and Accountability in Clinical Training*, Barry Edelstein and Ellen Berler, ed. New York: Plenum Press, 1986.

Queeney, Donna S. "The Role of the University in Continuing Professional Education," *Educational Record*, Vol. 65, No. 3 (Summer, 1984): pp. 13-17.

Smutz, Wayne D. et al. *The Practice Audit Model: A Process for Continuing Professional Education Needs Assessment and Program Development*. University Park, Pennsylvania: Continuing Professional Development Project, 1981. (Available from Commonwealth Educational System Stores, 7 J. Orvis Keller Building, University Park, PA 16802.)

Stern, Milton R. *Power and Conflict in Continuing Professional Education*. Belmont, California: Wadsworth Publishing Company, 1983.

Donna S. Queeney is Director of Planning Studies and Professor of Adult Education, The Pennsylvania State University. She frequently writes and speaks on various aspects of continuing professional education.

Institutional Models and Applications in Assessing Prior Learning

In this section we offer the reader a review of institutional models and policies that pertain to the assessment of prior learning. As is pointed out by Cabell and Hickerson, the models and policies developed within any particular institution must reflect its mission and commitment to its students. Before embarking on an implementation course, it must identify the resources—both human and financial—it can commit to the establishment of the program. A wide spectrum of U.S. colleges and universities offer opportunities for adults to demonstrate their prior learning. The examples given by Cabell and Hickerson reflect a good sample of these innovative institutions.

The last two chapters of this volume describe two of the many existing international efforts in the assessment of prior learning. Norman Evans focuses his attention on the advances made in England; and Robert Isabelle provides insight on the work in Quebec Canada. Both are indicative of a movement that is literally sweeping the globe. Educators, government policy makers, administrators, and industrialists alike are expressing the same compelling educational, economic, social and political reasons to acknowledge and accredit peoples' prior learning: to identify the strengths and creative powers of each individual, stimulating flexible learning and training alternatives and thereby create a world full of life-long learners.

In concluding with these two chapters, we would welcome readers' accounts of other emerging programs and opportunities. The prospects appear bright for continued growth, expansion and distinctive applications of the assessment process. We have vast opportunities to learn to enhance the educational and training options of the thousands of people around the world who need and seek new challenges for themselves, their communities and nations.

Chapter 9

Institutional Models: Whys and Hows of Prior Learning Assessment

Harriet Cabell and Jerry H. Hickerson

Why Assess Prior Learning?

A few years ago, John, a 37 year-old "retired" businessman and full-time student, asked his academic adviser if there were a way that he might accelerate the completion of his baccalaureate program. The adviser's report relates this sequel: "Aware that he had enrolled at the university intending to follow a traditional class route to his degree, I (J. Hickerson) asked him why. In his typically understated and matter-of-fact way, he volunteered that he already knew most of what had been covered in his first two business courses and, from reviewing the Catalog and talking informally with professors, believed that most of the next 30 hours of his concentration would follow a similar pattern. I knew that for 15 years before entering college he had purchased, developed, and sold what had become three thriving enterprises. And, for almost as long, he had pursued an interest in American history which had led him to read extensively and visit museums throughout the eastern United States. It was obvious to anyone who talked with him that John had more than a passing knowledge of business and certain epochs of American history. But, he now wondered, could he receive college credit for this learning? If so, how? And how much credit could he earn?"

"I had asked, "Why?" The answer was obvious to John, as it is to most adults under similar circumstances: 'I know a lot about this already — probably more than the typical student who has completed classes covering similar subject matter. Allow me the chance to prove it, give me credit for my college-level learning, and let me get on with my life!' For the faculty member who equates a degree with four years of successful responses to classroom instruction, however, the answer to the question is less certain."

Many excellent teachers question the quality (perhaps more, the coherence) of learning that students gain outside a classroom. Still, a routine part of the new-student orientation programs at most colleges is to attempt to place students into courses which best build on their abilities and "prior learning." Good teachers test, as well, to learn more about the knowledge and competence that students have brought with them in order "to tailor instruction to the capabilites and the interests of the students."[1] It is easier, in either case, to interpret the assessments of typical 18 or 19 year olds. They usually come to college with similar academic and social expectations and with various needs which the college program is designed to address. Their test scores have preceded them, from examinations taken at about the same time — the sorts of conditions that allow such tests to be reasonably reliable predictors of success in college for a homogeneous group of adolescents.

For the opposite reasons, proper placement of adult students into traditional academic programs is more difficult. They may have been away from formal education for decades. Their backgrounds and ways of learning are more diverse. Their learning may be fragmented, a piece here and a bit there. And they are unaccustomed to (and may resent or fear) taking standardized tests. Their high school test scores have virtually no predictive value, particularly for those who scored low, and tests normed for high school students but taken by adults for college admission seem to predict almost as little. Consequently, to place them in the appropriate levels of course and curriculum can be a problem. Some 1200 colleges in the United States, therefore, provide means for students to receive at least some college credit for what they already know — most often through selected standardized tests, such as those in the College-Level Examination Program (CLEP). (Chapter 3).

John's college — a large, highly regarded university in the Southeast — was proof of an axiom: the range of assessment opportunities provided by a college and the ways that the results of those assessments can be applied to the student's academic program are directly proportional to an institution's potential for serving adults

---

[1] Morris Keeton, "Assessing and Credentialing Prior Experience," *The Modern American College*, Arthur W. Chickering and Associates (Jossey-Bass Publishers, 1984), p. 631.

effectively. A number of ways to assess prior learning were in place, and John's academic program was sufficiently flexible to allow for all of his assessed prior learning to "count" toward graduation requirements. The service that the institution was able to render as a result of these considerations suggested another observation: colleges today which have responded to the needs and uniquenesses of non-traditional students through policy and program development geared to address them are maintaining their enrollments—and their reputations—and moving forward during a period of fewer traditional students, while some of those reluctant, or unable, to serve other than middle-class, 18-23 year olds are in a degree of crisis.

The changes made by John's college to accommodate hundreds of students with similar needs were hardly as drastic as those required to establish the Land Grant Colleges in the 1860s and 1890s in response to the need for applied research, or the "evening colleges" in response to the needs of greater numbers of working adults for postsecondary education following World War II.[2] The essential aims of American higher education have remained the same through these changes: the acquisition of knowledge, preservation of knowledge, transmission of knowledge, discovery of talents and aptitudes of learners, and the certification of educational achievement. The changes have tended to revolve around the questions of what knowledge is of most worth and how that knowledge can most effectively be transmitted and assessed.

While a handful of colleges, like Antioch and Goddard, have been known for innovative curricula and means of delivering education to nontraditional students for many years, it was not until the 1970s that states began to organize colleges with adult students as the primary focus. Studies on adult learners from the evening college movement and other sources provided much of the theory, and philanthropic foundations much of the incentive, for establishing such institutions as Empire State College (New York), Metropolitan State University (Minnesota), and Thomas A. Edison State College (New Jersey). Many more institutions, public and private alike, developed special programs for adults through new divisions or expansion of their continuing education units, while maintaining their traditional programs otherwise unaltered. A few organized to

---

[2] See John P. Dyer, *Ivory Towers in the Market Place: The Evening College in American Education* (Bobbs-Merrill Co., 1956), for an interesting apologetic for evening colleges during the early 1950s.

provide adult-oriented services within their traditional organizations and academic programs. Most, however, had concluded that it
was, in the words of Edison president George Pruitt, "impossible to
respond effectively to the learning requirements of two populations,
so different in their backgrounds and preparation, within the same
curriculum and policy context."[3]

Today, the challenge for colleges to change in response to the
increasing diversity of those needing higher education comes from
many quarters. To those involved in the administration of higher education, Arthur Chickering's *Modern American College*, suggests models
of reorganization to improve educational experiences for these "new"
students — diverse in age, educational purposes, background and
preparation, socio-economic status, and ethnicity. To those concerned
about accreditation, a recent Council on Postsecondary Accreditation
(COPA) publication — *Educational Quality and Accreditation* (subtitled,
"A Call for Diversity, Continuity and Innovation") — challenges institutions to (1) sharpen statements of mission and objectives to identify
intended educational outcomes, (2) develop additional effective means
of assessing learning outcomes and results, (3) use the self-evaluation
and peer review processes of accreditation as an integral part of ongo-
ing planning and institutional or programmatic change, and (4) incorporate in the planning process an examination of demographic and
technological changes as they relate to future societal needs.[4] To
department chairpersons and faculty, Allan Tucker states that a "deliberate development effort" should be undertaken to help faculty work
with the increasing number of learners with wide ranges of abilities,
interests, and life experiences — who "may have more experience than
the instructor and be as knowledgeable in some subjects . . . , [who]
often challenge time-tested and traditional ways of perceiving how
knowledge is organized . . . [and may] wish to be involved in educational decision making processes, such as needs assessment, goal setting, selection of content and method, and evaluation."[5]

The call for change seems urgent, because the current group of
adult students does not seem to be traveling on a passing band-

[3] George A. Pruitt, "The Adult Student and the Urban University," Keynote Address
at the Symposium on the Adult Learner, Winston-Salem State University, NC,
August 20, 1985.
[4] *Educational Quality and Accreditation* (COPA, One Dupont Circle N.W., Suite 305,
Washington, DC 20036, 1986), p. 7.
[5] Allan Tucker, *Chairing the Academic Department* (American Council on Education/Mac-
millan Publishing Co., 1984), pp. 123-24.

wagon. Simply stated, adults today need additional postsecondary education more than at any time in the past, and adults of the future may need it even more. Howard Bowen made the case nearly a decade ago that a modern, technically-oriented nation needs a well educated citizenry.[6] Similarly, Great Britain, with no traditional-student enrollment problem, has established policies to encourage adults to participate in postsecondary learning and training because it is perceived to be in the nation's best interest.[7] In America, the states oversee education with state colleges given autonomy to a degree determined by their respective state legislatures. Consequently, access to higher education designed to accommodate a wide range of needs and life situations in one's own state might well depend on the insight of a member of a Board of Regents or Board of Governors, an influential politician, or a dynamic academic leader, perhaps in a private college.

In the meantime, changing economic and social conditions are causing greater numbers of women, many with children and jobs, to seek educations for mobility into a variety of professions. Men and women alike are finding their jobs in jeopardy as a result of corporate reorganization or changing technology, triggering a need for further education. At the same time, they often find themselves locked out of opportunities for upward mobility, not because they lack knowledge or skill or competence, but because they lack a college diploma.[8] More than simply learning new skills, then, it is a college degree — official certification of success with a certain body and level of knowledge — that is becoming more highly valued among adults — and employers.

A problem that adults often face in achieving such a goal, however, is an organizational one. Many colleges (chiefly four-year colleges) still seem to lack incentives to reorganize to serve persons who would bring disparate backgrounds, variable attendance patterns, and various preferred ways to learn. Thus, at many colleges, students like John are still required to complete 120 to 130 credits by lis-

---

[6] Howard R. Bowen, *Adult Learning, Higher Education, and the Economics of Unused Capacity* (College Entrance Examination Board), 1980.

[7] Great Britain's directions in adult education are explained or implied in a number of documents, including *Into the 1990s* (Open University, 1986); *A New Training Initiative: An Agenda for Action* (Manpower Services Commission, December 1981); and *Continuing Education: Post-Experience Vocational Provision for Those in Employment*, A Paper for Discussion (Department of Education and Science, October 1980).

[8] Peter Meyer, *Awarding College Credit for Non-college Learning* (Jossey-Bass Publishers, 1976), p. 4.

tening to professors, as excellent as they might be, telling them much that they already know — except for a few lower division credits that might be earned through taking standardized tests. At many other colleges, though, they would find well conceived assessment services available and academic programs in place that consider assessed prior learning as an integral and logical part of the distribution requirements for a degree. A full-service institution that would accommodate adult students must include both assessment of learning already gained and a curriculum that focuses on the needs of older-than-typical students.

Ways Institutions Assess and Accommodate Prior Learning

By providing a variety of ways to assess previous learning for credit consideration, many postsecondary institutions are able to serve persons from a greater variety of backgrounds. As has been discussed elsewhere in this book, challenge examinations, standardized tests and the evaluation of licenses and certificates are increasingly being adopted and used.

The portfolio — a dossier of information, developed by the student under specific guidelines, about the individual's past experiences and accomplishments, accommodates many diverse learning styles.[9] Some adult-oriented programs, in fact, regard the development of a prior learning portfolio as so important a part of an adult's collegiate learning that it is required. A great amount of writing and organization, for example, are involved in completing such a document. Yet, those involved in portfolio programs suggest that there is much more. At Sinclair Community College, Barry Heermann found that the students participating in portfolio development "spoke of changes in self concept, a new sense of empowerment, and a heightened image as a learner."[10] "Empowerment," in particular, is a term frequently used by those involved in the assessment process to describe the key behavioral benefit that adults seem to gain as a

[9] Joan Knapp and Marianne Gardiner, "Assessment of Prior Learning: As a Model and in Practice," *Financing and Implementing Prior Learning Assessment*, Joan Knapp, ed., New Directions for Experiential Learning, No. 14, December 1981 (Jossey-Bass Publishers), p. 9.

[10] Barry Heermann, "Credit for Lifelong Learning Program — Sinclair Community College, Dayton, Ohio," Ibid., p. 100.

result of the portfolio development process. Cohen defines the concept as one of "the abilities of people to manage their lives, to recognize and meet their needs, and to fulfill their potential as creative, responsible, and productive members of society"[11] — aims for students often found in institutional mission statements.

Consequently, at a few colleges adults with particularly productive and academically enriched backgrounds can theoretically earn an entire degree, if so recommended by the faculty assessors. This scale of award, however, seldom happens, and institutions typically place limitations on credit that can be awarded through the portfolio assessment process. In reality, fewer than a third of the adult students at institutions providing a portfolio option typically receive such credit and, even where there is little or no limitation on credit, students normally receive about 17 semester hours of credit by this means. Still, the portfolio is regarded by those who use it as an important assessment tool for the information it yields about a student and the benefits that a student derives from developing a portfolio — a confidence supported by more than a decade of use in numerous colleges and studies by the Council for Adult and Experiential Learning (CAEL) and others. The state-of-the-art in ways of assessing prior learning and the practice of accommodating assessments into a nontraditional student's program is, therefore, not particularly new.

John's College: A Comprehensive Adult Degree Program Model

John, our 37 year-old with a rich out-of-class learning background, had already completed 45 hours of traditional course work — not unlike many adults, who transfer credits from earlier college experiences to new programs. Now he sought additional credit through development of a portfolio — an impressively packaged collection of essays, documents, and certificates related to his knowledge of business and history — that would be assessed by faculty members of appropriate academic departments. John was first, however, required to complete a short course in portfolio development. In it, he gained an understanding of his own preferred learn-

---

[11] Audrey Cohen, "Human Service," *The Modern American College*, op. cit., p. 514.

ing style through a theoretical model, based on Kolb's[12] work, which classifies preferred approaches to learning into four distinctive types: "concrete experience," "reflective observation," "abstract conceptualization," and "active experimentation." While John would use all four stages of learning in the development of his portfolio, "reflective observation" would be the stage most often employed. Building on these concepts, he was then led to consider what "significant learning experiences" meant at the college level and determine which aspects of his own learning were applicable to a portfolio — experiences which could be documented through certificates, licenses, and other means, and which provided learning outcomes and competencies that could be demonstrated in other ways. Using criteria for "college level learning" and guidelines for measurement and evaluation, he began to build his portfolio.

Finally, in addition to learning about how his portfolio would be evaluated, he was made aware of the broader implications of the portfolio as an assessment tool, identifying for him areas of his learning that might need attention and be strengthened through classes or independent study.

John developed an impressive portfolio. He met with faculty to discuss certain aspects of his learning and followed the portfolio experience with independent studies suggested by professors who were interested in working with him further. Ultimately, he received credit in accounting, management, marketing, and history totalling 40 semester hours. These credits were recorded on his transcript as specific university courses "passed" with a "prior learning" designation to identify the method by which the credits had been earned.

John's college was a university unit that had been established specifically for nontraditional students. This unit was helpful to him in several ways. Admission was based on proof of high school graduation and an interview — not the grades on aged high school or college transcripts, or standardized admissions tests. Placement tests were provided as advisement tools to give John and his advisor more information about his readiness for certain levels of study. And his academic program allowed him greater flexibility to meet the distribution requirements for a degree than did the prescribed programs created for traditional, more homogeneous students. He was in the process of completing his requirements in humanities, social sci-

---

[12] David A. Kolb, "Learning Style Inventory," (McBer and Co.), 1976.

ences, and natural sciences through the interdisciplinary courses offered in his division. He used the CLEP to meet his mathematics requirements. He would complete most of his major through his portfolio, conduct research through independent contracts, and use most of his 30 hours of electives to enhance his learning in history. All of the credits earned through his prior learning could, therefore, be awarded to one area or another of his program — as concentration, elective hours, or general education credits, if needed.

As a result of John's abilities and the program in which he was enrolled, he graduated in about three years with a Bachelor of Science degree (*magna cum laude*) and moved into a key management position with a growing firm. That he completed a more flexible interdisciplinary program with a "management science concentration," rather than a more prescribed "business major," has made no difference in his career, and his transcript effectively reflects the quality and extent of his academic background.

Mary Baldwin College

Mary Baldwin, a liberal arts college for women with approximately 900 students, enrolls over 300 women — and men — above the age of 32 in its Adult Degree Program (ADP), a nonresidential program which confers the Bachelor of Arts degree, employing individualized curricula designed to meet educational and career needs. Students attend an orientation session prior to matriculating into the program in order to become familiar with policies and procedures and to begin to develop individualized educational plans.

The ADP emphasizes a variety of learning experiences. Students are required to complete at least 36 course units from the five divisions of the college's liberal arts curriculum. Individualized learning contracts are also valued, a minimum of nine course units of contract learning being required of each student. And students may also seek credit through the use of prior learning portfolios.

Portfolios are presented for evaluation to Mary Baldwin faculty members or other approved resource persons, at a cost of $50-$100 to the student. Two assessors may be required for a comprehensive evaluation, and, occasionally, should the portfolio involve more than one discipline, other experts may be sought, with the possible result of a higher cost.

Students must be accepted, although not necessarily enrolled, in the ADP to have their prior learning portfolios considered for evaluation. There is no limit on the number of credits students may receive for prior learning, but prior learning alone may not be used to complete a baccalaureate degree. Moreover, credit may be awarded for learning which corresponds with that expected in courses taught residentially at Mary Baldwin or which does not, but the learning content must fall within the general purview of the liberal arts curriculum of the school. Engineering credit, for instance, would not be awarded.

Prior learning is awarded on a course-by-course, rather than a block or cluster, basis. Credit is designated on the official transcript as "P.L.," followed by the course equivalent title, or by an approved title for a nonequivalent course, and the amount of credit awarded.

The Core-Portfolio-Requirement Model

If John had lived in Southern California, he would have found a different approach to earning his degree. In 1976, the University of Redlands established the Alfred North Whitehead Center for Lifelong Learning, named for the English philosopher and mathematician whose early 20th century writings continue to interest and influence modern educators. There is, consequently, a degree of pride associated with involvement in the Center's programs, which include five Bachelors' and two Masters' curricula for "people who work." Adult undergraduates must complete 30-33 credits in a "core" of courses in the major, taken in "learning groups" (15 or more students registering for a particular class) in a traditional classroom setting (each meeting one evening per week for four hours at regional locations) — approaches which seem designed to foster group identity and quality control. Moreover, whether the academic major is Health Science, Management, Business Administration, or Liberal Studies, the second course taken by students is the same: Psychology 301, "Personal and Professional Assessment." Each student in the course is required to develop a "Life Learning Portfolio," which includes documentation of prior learning, a work autobiography, and specific proposals for consideration of learning that students wish to have evaluated for additional credit. Up to 40 units, distributed as needed and applicable to flexible distribution requirements, may be granted through this process upon completion of the core. John would have, therefore, had the opportunity, again, to earn much of the credit required for his degree through his portfolio — if he had been admissable. To enter the program, he would have needed to transfer, or earn at Redlands, 40 semester units of credit, with a minimum of 60 required for "regular" student status.

This requirement would have delayed his matriculation, and he might also have raised questions about being required to take courses in subjects in which he could already demonstrate considerable mastery. Nevertheless, institutions which use this approach consider classroom involvement with the faculty and the group support and identity gained in the learning groups as important features of their contributions to adults.

The Comprehensive Assessment Model

The fourth model is a hypothetical, albeit logical, extension of competency based programs, such as the one at Alverno College and, more recently, Northeast Missouri State. At such institutions, the abilities (competencies) expected of graduates are specified, and tests are administered to provide an assessment of which specified abilities are already possessed by each entering student — and, of course, which must yet be attained.

At Alverno, the curriculum has been developed around eight general competencies: communications, analysis, problem solving, valuing, social interaction, environment, citizenship, and aesthetic — with "performance" providing a ninth, non-required dimension. Each general competency typically includes six levels of depth or sophistication which must be achieved, if not assessed as having been attained, before a student can graduate. Various courses or other methods of study have been matched with each competency cell in this eight by six matrix, and students pursue the necessary study to achieve the levels of ability required. Alverno also provides among its academic offerings an adult-oriented weekend program, which includes the locally developed entry assessment activity required of all its students. It does not, however, use portfolios to assist in the assessment of competency attainment.

Theoretically, a competency or ability-based curriculum is ideally suited for the portfolio assessment process. Having the knowledge and specific levels of attainment valued by the college identified in discrete terms, prospective students could be expected to develop more "efficient" portfolios, focusing specifically on the required levels of expectation.

Educational leaders planning or providing competency-based programs should, therefore, consider the range of approaches necessary, and available, to assess the prior learning of prospective students most effectively. Will the methods used allow those from diverse backgrounds and with various preferred learning styles to demonstrate their abilities adequately, or will they assess well only a more narrowly prepared cohort? Will there, in any event, be time and assistance provided to help those who have been away from formal schooling for an extended period to prepare for the required assessments?

Other Models

Had John considered adult-oriented programs at other colleges, he would have found variations reflecting different approaches fostered by experimentation and local campus preferences. Program names might have included "Bachelor of Interdisciplinary (or Liberal, or Individualized, or Applied) Studies." There might have been differences in criteria for admission, approaches to assessment and assignment of prior learning credit, requirements in the distribution of courses for a degree, and modes of course delivery provided or allowable for meeting those requirements. Many programs would require applicants to have completed the equivalent of two years of college before being admitted (with prior learning credit sometimes considered as part of the equivalent). Prior learning assessment might be translated into courses, blocks of courses, or "competencies" — consistent with the program's policy on distribution requirements for a degree. Some programs would emphasize traditional or longer time-block classes, television or correspondence courses; others would use mentors to help the student develop a program and course delivery system uniquely tailored to his or her learning style and life situation.[13] The most comprehensive of these adult programs would accommodate persons whose jobs or other circumstances do not permit them to attend classes on a regular basis. Among these options would be distance-learning (external degree) programs through which students may complete degree requirements by virtually every possible means of earning credit, in accordance with the guidelines of the institution. In such programs, portfolio orientation courses, like others, might be offered on weekends or through a correspondence course like the one available through Ohio University.

---

[13] Mentoring is a key feature in personalizing higher education for students at Goddard College and for adults in the External Degree Program of Johnson State College.

The University of Alabama External Degree Program

A further model, that for external degrees, is traced by many back to the University of London, established by a royal charter in 1839. The University conferred degrees on all who passed prescribed examinations. The external degree programs in the United States, however, grew out of the intellectual and social forces of the turbulent 1960s. These programs tend to embody many practices especially geared for adult learners, and most of them have carefully thought-out portfolio assessment programs. Although enrollments in external degree programs have not achieved major proportions in higher education, the programs are significant to those persons whose geographic location, employment, or physical condition make attendance at a regular institution impossible. Such programs have documented excellent results with many students and, while not without criticism from some sectors, are building on research and experiences that are resulting in more shared practices among these "experimenting" institutions.

The University of Alabama External Degree Program (EXD) is part of the state's flagship university, which was founded in 1831. The 16,000 member student body is primarily the traditional residential-aged group. In 1970, however, a separate division, New College, was established to provide an opportunity for highly motivated undergraduates to create an individual education, utilizing the resources of the University. In 1971, the External Degree Program for adult learners was added as a department of the New College — both the College and its first department were based on the principles of CAEL, the New College being one of the original ten schools in the first CAEL project.

The External Degree Program is mandated to stay at around 500 students and to serve as an experimental unit with the expectation of exploiting successful innovations within and without the University. The Program has had great success, both in enrollment and student outcomes. With only word-of-mouth advertising, or through students' individual research on external degree programs, the Program has been oversubscribed since its beginning. More than 500 persons from every state in the Union have graduated from the program, more than half of them going on to graduate schools.

The EXD Program combines a variety of components that include flexible scheduling, recognition for prior learning, credit by examination, contract learning, and individualized degree planning. The EXD Program has a policy of open admissions, but students must be at least 22 years of age and have a high school diploma or a GED. They need come to the campus only once, for the beginning "Introduction to Adult Learning" seminar. Student characteristics tend to be remarkably consistent with national patterns. Students tend to be older, with a majority between 35 and 40 years of age; and most are white, married males who are employed full time and have children. Many exemplify the practice of recurring education, as the majority have prior college experience before enrolling in the program (Sazben & Sharp, 1978; Dice, 1982).

Prior to enrollment, students receive a handbook which includes information on goal-setting, degree planning, and an explanation of the special External Degree processes, such as out-of-class learning contracts and portfolio development. At the two-and-a-half day "Introduction to Adult Learning" seminar, the students meet in intensive advising sessions, learn how to individualize the curriculum, and begin the developmental process of developing a prior learning portfolio. After the seminar, students must return a degree plan, a sample learning contract, and a "significant learnings" outline.

In addition to using a prior learning guide, students are encouraged to enroll in a three-semester credit hour course entitled "Analytical Thinking From Experience." In this distance learning course, the learner utilizes the experiential learning cycle and analyzes prior experiences for college-level learning. A portfolio or a series of portfolios may be one product of the process. Many students enter the course in order to seek academic credit and to prepare a portfolio to shorten the time for the degree. Though they accomplish these goals, in the end the significant part of the experience is the process itself, as suggested by the following excerpt of a typical letter from a student:

> By taking the Contract Class in Portfolio Development I learned more than anything else that **I have a choice**. A choice in how I learn from these experiences. And most importantly how I choose to utilize **what** I learn. The whole concept of having this much freedom in my educational experience is more than a little unsettling. The idea of choice is exciting and brings with it that long forgotten spark of curiosity. For me, learning is once again a pleasure, something to be treasured and something to be con-

tinually renewed. With my new found sense of choice comes the examination of my life, particularly my professional life. I realize that I can utilize much of what I already know as a springboard for future contracts or portfolios. I understand that I am not limited in what I choose to learn more about.

In the EXD Program, broad parameters are set by the University, and students are encouraged to meet these requirements in a variety of ways. Students must have 12 hours in the humanities, 6 hours in the natural sciences, 6 hours in the social sciences, 32 hours in a depth study or major, and a 12 hour senior project. The remaining hours may be distributed among elements of the curriculum as needed to strengthen the student's program or for breadth in the elective area. Thirty-two hours must be completed under the auspices of the University of Alabama following admission to External Degree. These hours may include course attendance, assessment for prior learning, correspondence courses, and out-of-class learning contracts. Residence is established, not by being on campus, but by the completion of work under the guidance of University faculty. The student designs an interdisciplinary depth study or major with the assistance of the External Degree staff and advisors. The requirements of the major need not conform to those of any particular department but are based on an analysis of the knowledge that the student needs for an adequate program of study.

There is no limit to the amount of academic credit that can be earned by the portfolio process or by other assessment means. The credit may be applied to any area of the curriculum and may be a part of the residency requirement. Students must add to their previous learning with at least nine new hours in their depth study and the senior project.

Many External Degree students receive large amounts of academic credit through the assessment process. In an unpublished study, McAllister evaluated 41 graduates from 1985-86. Through the portfolio assessment process, 21 earned over 25% of the 128 hours needed for graduation. Seven of these graduates earned over 50% of the total needed for graduation. At the same time, 15 members of the group earned no academic credit through the portfolio process.

In the New College EXD Program, portfolios are evaluated by faculty who are experts in the academic area being assessed. The students are encouraged to know the University of Alabama faculty, and often new, more advanced learning results at the suggestion of the faculty member who evaluates the prior learning credit.

Upon completion of a portfolio, the student sends it to the External Degree Office, where it is reviewed by an advisor. If all the steps of the portfolio process as outlined by *Principles of Good Practice* and other references are in order, the portfolio is sent to a selected faculty expert. The faculty member reviews the document and makes one of three basic choices:

1. The learning is of college level and worthy of academic credit.

2. The learning represented is not of college level and is not worthy of academic credit.

3. The learning represented needs additional work to be of college level; additional information is needed before the faculty member can make a judgment; or the faculty member wishes a telephone or face-to-face interview with the student.

The latter choice is the one most commonly made, but the majority of those who submit a portfolio for academic credit do receive academic credit.

There is little formal preparation given to faculty assessors. They are given informal tutoring by the EXD advisors; occasionally, seminars and workshops are provided. A group or team approach is not used unless the faculty member requests additional assistance from colleagues or an area is particularly complex or of a very interdisciplinary nature.

Occasionally faculty report that the assessment process improves the quality of their own teaching. One faculty member said, "Before evaluating a portfolio, in my classes I tried to tell the students to read the text, attend my lectures, and take the tests." He then confessed: "Until I evaluated a portfolio, I never really thought about what I expected the students to know, or how well they should know it, or what they should be able to do after taking my class."

If students disagree with a faculty member's credit recommendation, they may petition for a re-evaluation of their portfolios, and occasionally this re-evaluation happens. A written policy with procedural steps is available upon request from the EXD Office.

Credit may be awarded in various ways: for specific course credits, as a block of credit, or in a particular discipline. The course equivalency is the most common and usual method because of the nature of the institution and the use of the faculty-expert model. Occasionally faculty members recommend blocks of credit—for instance, 12 hours of credit in the area of "Newspaper Management," or credit for a particular discipline; e.g., six hours in Business Management.

While an external degree program is not the right model for every institution or for every student, it is one that provides a framework in which assessment by portfolio is a natural component. Because of the portfolio assessment program's existence at Alabama, a grandmother was able to accelerate her academic goals just prior to her retirement and, after earning over 50 semester hours for her wealth of learning experience, subsequently completed two Master's degrees. At the other end of the age continuum, an unmotivated 18 year old, in whom a professor saw talent and potential in journalism, developed a portfolio for assessment of his journalism experience, earning himself six hours of credit and causing a change in his perspective on college, a perspective which contributed to his graduating with honors. The New College External Degree Program, with more than a decade of success for students, institutions, and society, as well as other programs such as those identified above, is a testimony to the value of flexible degree models and a clue that assessment of prior learning in general is a viable option for thousands of adults who otherwise would be denied a chance for recognition of what they have accomplished.

Designing an Appropriate Program Model

Each college or university which undertakes a prior learning assessment service will choose from numerous program models to create a combination of features which best fits the goals and circumstances of that particular institution.

The designers need to understand the various programs and many different assessment options before making a decision about which is best for them. Likewise, faculty who are involved in assisting in such programs or are on committees studying the feasibility of alternative programs for their campuses must ask similar questions. Publications, such as *Earn College Credit for What You Know*, offer assistance to students and faculty alike through suggestions like the following (pp. 29-30) (the questions are addressed to a student):

1. Does your institution give credit or recognition for credits earned through portfolio-assisted assessment or the assessment of experiential learning?

2. If so, does the institution have a limit on the number of credits you may earn by this method?

3. May credits earned through your assessment apply to any aspect of your degree program or only to a selected portion; free electives, for example?

4. Will credits awarded for your prior learning be applied to your degree program immediately or only after particular course requirements have been met?

5. When should you begin the assessment process?

6. What are the fees?

7. What printed materials, guidelines, and forms are you to use?

8. What personal assistance does the institution provide, such as workshops, advisors, or a course on assessment?

9. Is there a time restriction on the length of time in which you must complete your portfolio or assessment?

10. Who will assess your portfolio after it is developed?

11. How and by whom are credit recommendations made?

12. Can you appeal a credit recommendation decision?

Options on Crediting

In *Earn College Credit for What You Know* (1985, p. 31), Simosko points out that students are generally requested by institutions of higher education to articulate what they know within the context of one of three primary models: the College Course Model, the Learning Components Model, or the Block Credit Model. These may be described as follows (again the models are addressed to the student):

The College Course Model requests that you equate your knowledge to specific college courses, using college catalog descriptions or course syllabi to guide you. The Credit for Lifelong Learning Program, Sinclair Community College, Dayton, Ohio, utilizes this method, as does the Adult Degree Program (ADP) at Mary Baldwin College in Staunton, Virginia.

The Learning Components Model requires you to cluster your college skills and knowledge in a particular academic discipline, not limiting yourself to a particular college course description. Delaware Community College, Dover, Delaware, and Alverno College, a private Catholic college in Milwaukee, employ this model.

The Block Credit Model requires you to consider your college level learning in light of depth and breadth of knowledge obtained by someone who has graduated from college and is employed in the field of the claim. This model may be one of the options for several institutions and is sometimes utilized by New College at the University of Alabama and Empire State College, New York.

Essential components of the models tend to blur with a vast array of actual institutional arrangements. Each model has its strengths as well as its weaknesses, and each has its own proponents. Numerous program variations representing the models are described in the CAEL literature and in readily available guides such as *Bear's Guide to Non-Traditional Study*. Preference for one model over another may be related to the personal academic policies of the planners rather than to the particular merits of the model itself. For example, Simosko directs the student by saying, "If your institution or the program in which you are enrolled requires you to match your knowledge to a specific college course, much of the burden of requesting the right amount will be lifted from your shoulders" (p. 76).

On the other hand, Knapp writes, "If the learner is enrolled in an institution that has competency based education . . . he or she has a decided advantage . . . a competency based program is an easier task than matching skills to course requirements" (1981, p. 16).

At the same time, Cabell (1986) in an unpublished speech to educators in Alaska advocated, "Prior learning rarely fits into a specific course model. Students are encouraged to think through their non-collegiate learning by utilizing the experiential learning cycle: to describe the concrete experience; to reflect upon the experience; to relate the experience to abstract knowledge, methodologies, principles, theories; and to synthesize the experiences." In summary, there is apparently no best model, but the different models fit different types of learning, different kinds of students, and different institutions.

Transcribing

After the prior learning is assessed and evaluated, it must be recorded. An official transcript is the primary method for communicating the learning to a third party. Despite the best efforts of dedicated organizations and professionals, including CAEL and the American Association of Collegiate Registrars and Admissions Officers (AACRAO), there seems to be no clear consensus in the area of transcribing the learning. In the earlier survey, transcription was the area of greatest disagreement among participants. Over 50% of the respondents used traditional course letters and numbers, 25% a narrative description, and 29% transcribed the learning as a block of credit (Cabell, 1980, p. 3). A number of different designations for the transcript were listed, including prior learning, experiential learning, college equivalent credit, credit by evaluation, life experience credit, special assessment, and a special course number. In addition, in its application to degree programs, prior learning assessment credit is sometimes treated differently from traditional course credit. The external degree program at Eckerd College in St. Petersburg, Florida, reports that it does not officially record the prior learning credit earned unless the student graduates from the institution.

Credit Limitations

The majority of institutions place limits on the amount of prior learning credit that can be earned (Kintzer, p. 38), but from available data, there is inconclusive evidence as to the comparative prevalence of policies which discriminate between lower and upper division credit, or exclude one or the other. Institutions do insist that college credit be awarded only for college-level learning, most often related to subject matter taught at some regionally accredited college, not necessarily their own (Cabell, 1980, p.2). Institutions dedicated to part-time students, as well as junior or community colleges, often have written articulation and transfer agreements with neighboring institutions. Institutions that do not specialize in experiential learning credit often have no written policy on the subject; and if they do, it is, "generally rigid, stipulating a credit maximum" (p. 38). The credit that will be accepted is restricted to credit under carefully drawn guidelines.

It is obvious that institutions entering into portfolio assessment need to be aware of the differences among practices at various institutions and that the institutions should develop policies that communicate to students a clear and fair method for reporting the learning.

Using the Portfolio in Evaluation

In assessing the learning and in using the portfolio to evaluate the learning, judgments by faculty are essential, not only concerning the quality and amount of learning, but also on the appropriateness of the learning for meeting certain curricular or degree requirements. The evidence of the learning to be judged is often a combination of the portfolio and in-person or telephone interviews between faculty and students, with a performance appraisal or product evaluation frequently added. The assessment itself tends to follow either the subject matter expert model or a team approach with diverse fields of expertise among the faculty, and with widely varying preparation from the use of written guidelines, individualized training, workshops, or a combination of these measures to almost nothing. There is evidence that the approach itself often influences credit recommendations. According to Spille (1980, p. 18), team approaches tend to be quite conservative with experts unwilling to recommend credit beyond amounts with which they are completely comfortable. While there are exceptions to this pattern, including the Statewide Testing and Assessment Center (STAC) in New Jersey at Thomas A. Edison State College, generally each institution tends to develop its own version of assessment, a version dependent upon the rationale of the program, the faculty at the institution, and the politics of the time.

Empire State College, the non-residential college of the State University of New York, uses a faculty evaluator to make an informed judgment on a limited portion of the evidence of learning presented as a part of a total portfolio (Serling, 1980, p. 48). An assessment committee consisting of three or more faculty members and an associate dean, who is not necessarily an expert in a particular area, receives the information of the evaluation as a part of a more holistic judgment of the student's degree plan and the competencies represented. At Edison State College, a portfolio is regularly assessed by a faculty consultant, usually a faculty member who teaches in a relevant field at one of New Jersey's colleges or universities. Rarely do the practices vary greatly, but the process of assessment is complicated by the personal nature of the portfolio, which assumes that no two portfolios can ever be the same.

Present Views

While differences in the mechanics of adult-oriented programs are common, practitioners generally agree that the assessment of prior learning and the use of the assessment information to help students with academic planning and credit attainment are essential. Likewise, those who use portfolios to facilitate assessment are confident of the validity and power in the approach. As James Harrington of Mary Baldwin College states the case: "We view it as imperative that a program which claims to serve adult learners have some device for identifying, assessing, and recognizing what they already know. It serves an advising purpose, a credit-generating purpose, and a recruiting purpose, as well. We also feel strongly that the portfolio process is superior to other means of assessment because it is itself a learning process and it engages faculty judgment more directly than do other means."[14]

Why, then, do institutions place the limitations that they do on credit for prior learning by adults, even in programs designed to serve an adult culture? It is no doubt philosophy more than mission, sometimes politics more than philosophy. Two major factors seem to enter into institutional choices as to the amount of credit permitted for prior learning: a) the presence of abuses by unscrupulous or incompetent persons in this field, and b) the concern to place an institution's own distinctive stamp upon any degree it awards.

It is most important, from the perspectives of advocates for fair treatment of adult learners, that legitimate programs for the crediting of extra-collegiate learning distance themselves from degree mills and other abusers of the academic currency.

The most appropriate way to do so is to put in place clearly articulated standards and well-monitored processes for competent assessors applying sound assessment processes, not to place arbitrary limits on the amount of credit that may be earned.

The concern to put the institution's stamp upon a degree program is especially appropriate for colleges and programs that are truly distinctive. Regarding this concern, the key point is that the distinctiveness should be clearly defined, and the means of assuring its achievement in a graduate should then be appropriate to that end. Normally that assurance cannot be as well assured by an arbitrary requirement of residency as by means that are more directly related to the distinctive contribution that the institution intends to make to the student's development. Assessment of the student's development can serve as a check, both on whether the traditional means are working, and on whether an adult has attained that distinctive development in other ways.

A third factor often bears on the concern to limit credit for nontraditional ways of learning; viz., the institution's tolerance for inno-

---

[14] James J. Harrington, Prior Learning Assessment Survey, July 17, 1986.

vation. Among colleges and universities, there is a wide range in the degree of tolerance for innovation. It derives, at least in part, from the beliefs of the power structure about what a college should be and how "quality" can be ensured (not necessarily "assured," which would require measurement). The range of acceptability is demonstrated through the number of ways that an institution provides for diverse learners to achieve its standards for an academic degree. The range taken is from within the extremes of the continuum of academic practices, from a single common curriculum to a smorgasbord; from a single way to provide teaching and credit for all students alike to credit provided through methods acceptable only to the student; from no credit for prior learning to a degree completed through prior learning. But these are extremes. It is the range of tolerance between the extremes — the search for, as Dewey put it, "the organic connection between education and personal experience"[15] — that is important to an institution's exploration into the consideration of programs that would serve adults effectively.

Conclusion

There are some key variables which seem to influence the policies of colleges toward assessing prior learning for credit: mission, as reflected by an institution's orientation to traditional or non-traditional students and disposition toward credentialing as a function of the academic program; philosophy of education, as reflected by the range of means provided for students to prove their abilities or gain additional knowledge; and the economics of enrollment management. For those institutions electing to provide comprehensive services for adult students, a number of ways have been developed for ascertainment of learning already achieved, and a variety of program models established that will translate such assessments into credit toward an academic degree, an important goal for a growing number of adult students today. An increasingly popular method for assisting the assessment of prior learning is portfolio development, which provides credit opportunities for students of diverse backgrounds and learning styles. In spite of the differences among institutions in credit allowable for portfolios, there are many similarities in process

---

[15] John Dewey, *Experience and Education* (Macmillan Co., Collier Books, 1938), pp. 19-20.

and outcome, widely acknowledged by those who administer effective portfolio programs:

1. Students receive an orientation to portfolio development — often in the form of a course for credit.

2. Faculty are used as the assessors (usually following an orientation to portfolio assessment) — because they possess the expertise necessary to judge the level of learning demonstrated by students in their disciplines.

3. Credit is awarded as individual course equivalents or for learning contracts or as blocks of credit (such as "humanities"), according to the distribution requirements of the academic program — equating evidence of learning documented in the portfolio and quality of presentation to courses in the college, or using a point system related to the level and degree of competency attained.[16]

4. Transcription of credit is consistent with courses in the college catalog, insofar as possible, often with a designation indicating that credit was gained through assessment — making the student's record understandable but not exotic.

5. The adult becomes empowered as a learner and person through the process — an observation made by most of those involved with students who participate in portfolio development.

Finally, the portfolio process, as an effective means of assessing knowledge and skills of prospective students, can add an important dimension to competency-based programs and to counseling and curriculum planning in mentoring programs.

---

[16] George Mason University faculty use the form on the following page when determining points for portfolio credit (18-20 points equating to four credits).

GEORGE MASON UNIVERSITY
· Bachelor of Individualized Study, Division of Continuing Education
EXPERIENTIAL LEARNING: COMPETENCY EVALUATION FORM

Name of Student _____ SS# _____ BIS Concentration _____

Description of General Competency: _____

LEVEL OF COMPETENCY:

I. Knows and Comprehends _____

II. Can Apply _____

III. Can Analyze, Synthesize & Evaluate _____

IV. Can Use Analysis, Synthesis & Evaluation _____

LEVEL OF COMPETENCY	Student has demonstrated the competency in question:				
	Not at all	At a below average level	At an average level	At an above average level	At or near the highest level
	1	2	3	4	5
I					
II					
III					
IV					

Information for evaluation acquired from the following sources:

_____ Interview _____ Observation
_____ Written Materials _____ Written Test
_____ Student Narrative
_____ Third Party Testimony

Faculty Evaluator _____

Jobs(s) or experience during which student learning took place (include dates) _____

Signature of Evaluator _____

Department _____

BIS/DCE/1-82

References

AAHE Bulletin, 36 (February 1984), focus on Alverno College.

Cabell, Harriet. *Licenses and Certificates*. Columbia: CAEL, 1980.

CAEL News, Council for the Advancement of Experiential Learning, Vol. 8, No. 6, July 1985.

Cross, Patricia K. *Lifelong Learning: Purposes and Priorities*. CAEL.

Expert Assessment of Experiential Learning — A CAEL Handbook. Columbia: CAEL, 1977.

Fugate, Mary; and MacTaggart, Terrence. Managing the Assessment Function, *Cost-Effective Assessment of Prior Learning*. San Francisco: Jossey-Bass, Inc., Vol. 19, 1983, pp. 27-43.

Heermann, Barry (Ed.). *Personal Computers and the Adult Learner.* San Francisco: Jossey-Bass, Inc., 1986.

Heermann, Barry; Lowe, William; and Saltman, Lenore. Program Initiation and Implementation: Three Diaries of Practice, *Financing and Implementing Prior Learning Assessment*. San Franciso: Jossey-Bass, Inc., Vol. 14, 1981, p. 95.

Implementing a Program for Assessing Experiential Learning, Ed., Warren W. Willingham and Hadley S. Nesbitt. CAEL, January 1976.

Keeton, Morris T.; and Tate, Pamela J. (Eds.). *Learning by Experience — What, Why, and How*. San Francisco: Jossey-Bass, Inc., Vol. 1, 1978.

Kintzer, Frederick C. Problems in Awarding and Transferring Experiential Learning Credit, *Transferring Experiential Credit*. San Francisco: Jossey-Bass, Inc., Vol. 4, 1979, p. 37.

Knapp, Joan; and Gardiner, Marianne. Assessment of Prior Learning: As a Model and in Practice, *Financing and Implementing Prior Learning Assessment*. San Francisco: Jossey-Bass, Inc., Vol. 14, 1981, pp. 7-31.

Martorana, S.V.; and Kuhns, Eileen. The Politics of Control of Credit for Experiential Learning, *Transferring Experiential Credit*. San Francisco: Jossey-Bass, Inc., Vol. 4, 1979, pp. 1–14.

Menson, Elizabeth; Mark, Michael; and Heermann, Barry. *Ohio University Lifelong Learning Programs*. Athens: Ohio University Independent Study, 1980.

Opportunities for College Credit: A CAEL Guide to Colleges and Universities. Columbia: CAEL, 1986.

Publication Manual of the American Psychological Association. G & C Merriam Co., 1975.

Sabin, William A. *The Gregg Reference Manual*. Gregg Div./McGraw-Hill Book Co., 1977.

Simosko, Susan. *Earn College Credit for What You Know*. Washington, DC: Acropolis Books Ltd., 1985.

Spille, Henry, et. al. *Assuring High Standards, Quality Control, and Consistency*. San Francisco: Jossey-Bass, Inc., Vol. 7, 1980, p. 7.

Strange, John. Credit for Learning Gained in Life and Work Experience, *Developing New Adult Clienteles by Recognizing Prior Learning*. San Francisco: Jossey-Bass, Inc., Vol. 7, 1980, p. 37.

Women's External Degree Program. Saint Mary-of-the-Woods College. Saint Mary-of-the-Woods, IN.

Special thanks to the following for their survey responses and other contributions:

L. Ann Bielawski, Edison State College, Trenton, NJ

Joan Byrne, Metropolitan State University, Minneapolis, MN

Patricia Dice, New College, The University of Alabama, University, AL

Georgine Dluzak, Alverno College, Milwaukee, WI

Wilfred G. Hamlin, Goddard College, Plainfield, VT

James J. Harrington, Adult Degree Program, Mary Baldwin College, Staunton, VA

Kathleen McGuinness, George Mason University, Fairfax, VA

Susan Mancuso, Whatcom Community College, Bellingham, WA

Michael Mark, Adult Learning Services, Ohio University, Athens, OH

Joanna Noel, External Degree Program, Johnson State College, Johnson, VT

Vera Shelton, Salem College, Winston-Salem, NC

James Waddell, Whitehead Center for Lifelong Learning, University of Redlands, Redlands, CA

Jerry H. Hickerson is Assistant Vice Chancellor for Continuing Education and the Graduate Center and Professor of Education at Winston-Salem State University where he also teaches curriculum development and advanced grammar. He is North Carolina Regional Manager for CAEL and is involved on numerous committees for the Association for Adult and Continuing Education and the North Carolina Adult Education Association.

Harriet W. Cabell, is a speaker, trainer, educator, and consultant who has conducted programs nationwide and abroad for a variety of public and private audiences. Among those audiences are the National Conference of Community Service Credit Union Councils, the Alabama Women in Banking, the Central Michigan Banking School, the North Carolina Continuing Educators, the National Shorthand Reporters Association, and over sixty colleges and universities. Her training sessions focus on relevant, practical "how to" skills and techniques which show others how to achieve their potential.

Chapter 10

Prior Learning Assessment in the United Kingdom: Institutional Models[1]

Norman Evans

There is no doubt that the assessment of experiential learning is becoming widely practiced in the United Kingdom (UK). Institutions of many different types are joining in. This chapter is intended to provide a distillation of current experience and to offer examples of different models. As more schemes evolve, there will be more examples to draw on, and more to say about the assessment of experiential learning in the UK. For the present, this account states more or less where we are. Given the speed of development in the past four years, it is clear that during the next four years there is bound to be a very different story to tell.

This chapter is based mainly on practice in the assessment of experiential learning undertaken in educational institutions with the aim of facilitating academic access and progression. Similar methods may be used to assess experiential learning in relation to vocational retraining and updating and for career development.

Background

The assessment of experiential learning became a serious business for academia in the mid-1970s in the USA. In the UK, from 1980 on, work on the assessment of experiential learning has been initiated by the Policy Studies Institute, funded by the Wates Foundation, the Further Education Unit, the Council for National Academic

---

[1] This chapter has been adapted from *Assessing Experiential Learning*, Norman Evans, published by the Further Education Unit (FEU), 1987 in Great Britain.

Awards, and more recently, the Manpower Services Commission. Initially all of the work, which occurred in several different parts of the country, drew heavily on the American experience. Funds were obtained from the W. K. Kellogg Foundation's Project LEARN through the Council for Adult and Experiential Learning (CAEL) to establish the British-American Scholars Exchange Program. In addition some of the publications of CAEL remain invaluable for insights into the theory and practice of assessing experiential learning. In addition, the Experiential Learning Network, organized through the Policy Studies Institute, has made extensive use of visiting American experts, both in regular meetings and at three national conferences.

However, things are now at a stage when we in the UK have significant experience of our own to draw on. There is the same starting point as in the United States for all these developments: reflection on experience. In different kinds of institutions and for different purposes, tutors in further and higher education have set about devising what they see as the best way of putting programs for the assessment of experiential learning at the service of their students. Procedures have been tried out, refined and tried again. There are strong similarities and differences among the various attempts which have been made. But, overall, the reports by the tutors responsible for work with students represent a comprehensive testing of the general proposition that the assessment of experiential learning can bring a potent, even arresting additional dimension to the education and training of adults.

These contributions make it abundantly clear that if the assessment of prior learning has as its main aim the facilitating of access and progression, then the preparation of portfolios by itself is not enough. For portfolios of experiential learning to lead to the actual assessment of the learning, there has to be shared understanding and collaboration between tutors working at different levels, in different disciplines, and in many cases among institutions. What follows is a summary of some of the case studies which serve to indicate the nature and application of the assessment of prior learning in different UK contexts.

Case Studies–A Summary

The first course in the UK on the assessment of experiential learning was offered jointly at Thames Polytechnic and Goldsmiths' College of the University of London in 1982 under the title 'Making

Experience Count.' From 1983 onwards, the two institutions provided their own Making Experience Count (MEC) courses
separately.

Thames Polytechnic

Making Experience Count is a 33-week course, running for two
hours once a week, offered by the Continuing Education Unit. The
course aims to provide opportunities for men and women to conduct
a systematic reflection upon their experience as a means of deciding
what to do next. The course aims to build confidence and to enable
people to make more informed choices about their futures.

Recruitment is through the Continuing Education Unit's usual
distribution of leaflets and pamphlets, and through Open House
exploratory meetings held in September of each year. An important
vehicle for these activities is a shop in a busy precinct run by the
Greenwich Educational and Training Advice Service. Latecomers
may join the course up to Christmas, if tutors and students think it
makes sense to do so.

The participants in MEC courses are predominantly women,
some of whom are unemployed, many of whom are second-chance
returners. Most have slender formal educational qualifications.
None has the formal requirements for entry to degree courses. Men
tend to fall into the same educational category, and are usually
unemployed.

Making Experience Count takes as its content the life and work
experience of its student members. The course uses themes such as
"childhood," "organizing," and "family photographs," to stimulate
reflection on experience, which is then complemented by suggested
reading. The course is conducted through a mixture of group discussions and personal tutorials. Considerable "homework" and
written work is involved, as a result of which basic skills can develop
considerably. Each student is encouraged to compile a portfolio of
learning as he or she goes along.

Students end up with a learning portfolio, containing descriptions of key experiences, statements of what they claim to have
learned from those experiences, and evidence to support those
claims. Students can use their portfolios to support applications for
entry to degree-level courses, to access courses, and for
employment.

Goldsmiths' College

The Goldsmiths' course, like that at Thames Polytechnic, bases its content on the experience of students. It uses themes such as "schooling," or "working lives," as triggers for recollecting experience and makes use of the same mixture of group discussion and compilation of individual portfolios. What happens to the students during their time in the course is broadly similar to what happens to those at Thames Polytechnic.

But Goldsmiths' recruitment comes from the general advertising and admission procedures of the Department of Adult and Community Education, and therein lies the first difference. Unlike Thames, this is not an open access course. Formal application forms have to be submitted. The likely applicants are interviewed and screened for a requisite level of basic skills. So the course is selective, with a formality about the admission procedures which contrasts interestingly with the methodological style of the course itself.

The second notable difference is that, as Goldsmiths' is a constituent college of the University of London, its rules and regulations for first degree admissions present more hurdles to be cleared by "unqualified" applicants than do those of the Council for National Academic Awards, under which Thames Polytechnic conducts its academic work. In these circumstances access to higher education can not rely solely on portfolio assessment, and a wider range of outcomes was envisaged for the Goldsmiths' course. This policy is reflected in the final section of the case study report. As a result, portfolios were used to support applications for admission to degree level or access courses, or to obtain support for further training from an employer. For a number of participants, however, the value of portfolio preparation lay primarily in the way in which the experience had widened or changed their educational horizons.

Hackney College

Like Thames Polytechnic and Goldsmiths' College, Hackney College, beginning in 1983, developed its courses and the assessment of experiential learning for men and women who were at the threshold of postsecondary school study and were wondering whether they fit it or it fit them. But whereas to many of the students taking the Making Experience Count courses at Thames and Goldsmiths' a degree course is a reasonable next step, this fit is true for a smaller number of students at Hackney College. Hackney tends to attract students with a wide variety of expectations and attainments and does not teach degree courses itself. This feature is another institutional factor which influences the handling of the assessment of experiential learning.

Hackney College offers portfolio assessment of experiential learning in two ways. One is as a component of an Access B. Ed. course. The other is as a free-standing, voluntary workshop, offered on a drop-in basis, with a weekly session of two hours.

The aim of the portfolio component in the Access B. Ed. course is to help students bring together various parts of the course concerned with child development, and set these ideas against a systematic reflection on their own childhood experiences.

The workshop is intended to provide students with an opportunity to use portfolio preparation to provide them with a framework for self-assessment, for confidence-building, and for extended career guidance and planning. The portfolio is also intended to support applications to other courses, to offer admission tutors a record of students' knowledge and skill, and to help strengthen applications for employment.

The Hackney two-year experience demonstrates that the principles and methodology on which systematic reflection on experience are based can be used confidently with men and women of different abilities, at different stages of development, and with different expectations, because the assessment of experiential learning can serve them all equally well.

Vauxhall College

Accreditation at Vauxhall College is a 21-hour a week course, lasting 24 weeks. It has five elements: communication and study skills, orientation to further and higher education, single subjects such as sociology, a field placement, and portfolio preparation.

The original recruitment was through an open evening, advertised in the local press, to publicize and explain the course. Further advertising was through leaflets sent to community and career guidance centers. Selection for admission is by formal application and interview.

The course is designed for older men and women with few formal educational qualifications, starting out on further study, with particular consideration for encouraging and supporting students from ethnic minorities. Women have predominated. The course is designed as an alternative entry route to study in the social sciences, including degree courses.

The course aims to use portfolio preparation to integrate five separate parts of the course, and provide a cumulative record of attainment in each of the five parts. Achievement is recorded in competence terms, enabling students to match their attainments with required entry competences, which have been determined through negotiation with admission tutors to social science degrees. These records concentrate on evidence of ability to cope with a degree course. Students then use their portfolios to support their applications for entry to courses in polytechnics and colleges.

Hillcroft College

Hillcroft College is not concerned with access. It has no need to do so, as a small residential college for women who are mature full-time students following a course of preparation for degree level work.

The College reckoned that if it could get a better understanding of how its students viewed their previous life and work experience, and how they thought it related to what they were to study, teachers would be better equipped to match their courses to the women who came to them. So in 1981 an experiential learning questionnaire was circulated to all incoming students, covering those three areas. This instrument has been used each year subsequently. In this way, knowledge of the experiential learning the women students brought with them has been seen as a tool for curriculum design.

Trying to develop programs for part-time students, Hillcroft also planned weekend short courses as part of a career and life planning exercise. Part of the content of these courses was information about opportunities for further study or training; but the starting-point was the experience, knowledge, and skills the women had accumulated already. So experiential learning provided the arena in which plans for the future could be considered.

City of Sheffield Polytechnic

Sheffield Polytechnic's work with the assessment of experiential learning has yet a different focus. The work began in 1984 as a voluntary experimental project in collaboration with the National Coal Board. The project set out to articulate the knowledge and skill acquired by non-graduate junior and middle managers from their work, combined with what they had learned from previous study, and to assess their academic attainments against the requirements of award-bearing courses in Business Studies and Management. Here was a different student clientele—men and women in full-time employment—which required a different kind of "course"—a small number of group meetings and tutorials with participants doing their portfolio work substantially on their own, all off-campus.

Sheffield Polytechnic demonstrates that the assessment of experiential learning can offer a valuable service to employees and employers in relation to staff appraisal procedures, and supportive evidence in relation to progression in employment as well as admission to award-bearing courses.

Heriot-Watt University

Heriot-Watt University is different again. There, the experiential learning of experienced and qualified civil engineers is drawn on to improve the appropriateness, and so the quality, of provision for continuing professional development for experienced civil engineers, most of whom are seeking chartered status.

Experiential learning is approached through a range of different activities: extended individual interviews and workshops in the workplace. These activities are designed to enable each individual course participant to draw out and use learning acquired from professional work experience.

These methods are used to replace traditional continuing professional development or continuing professional education for engineers by a provision which is related explicitly to individual needs. The assessment of experiential learning has a diagnostic function, and enables participants to identify areas of learning required to advance their development. Strong and encouraging responses from both civil engineers and their employers mean that this work is expanding.

Middlesex Polytechnic

In Middlesex Polytechnic, interest in the assessment of experiential learning arose from the established practice of granting academic credit in respect of previously acquired knowledge and skills to mature students who were already enrolled on the Diploma of Higher Education and Combined Studies degree within the Modular Scheme. Interest quickened when the Polytechnic devised a modular scheme of some 450 units in 30 subject areas, and wanted to find ways of enabling students to complete a part-time degree as rapidly as possible.

Middlesex Polytechnic uses the assessment of experiential learning as a means of awarding academic credit retrospectively to mature students enrolled on degree-level courses validated by the Council for National Academic Awards. Preparation for assessment is conducted through two or three personal tutorials and two or three group meetings. This process puts on a coherent basis the awarding of credit for uncertified learning which is equivalent to degree level work.

A Typology of Aims and Outcomes

These summaries show that in the provision for the assessment of experiential learning the UK has had a variety of aims and outcomes in diverse institutions and settings. The range covered by these case studies comprises the identification and assessment of experiential learning in order to offer:

- Guidance and counseling—exemplified in the Hillcroft weekend short courses, and in some measure in the courses at Hackney College and Goldsmiths' College.

- Orientation and access to further study—exemplified in the Vauxhall College Accreditation course, and at Hackney College, Thames Polytechnic and Goldsmiths' College.

- Advanced academic or professional standing—exemplified at Middlesex and Sheffield Polytechnics and by Heriot-Watt University.

It is anticipated that as awareness of the methodology increases, new applications and uses will be found for the assessment of experiential learning. Indeed much progress has been made; much more remains to be done.

Norman Evans has worked in a variety of sections in the field of education. He was Head Master of Senecre Secondary School in Kent and Principle of Bishop Lonsdale College of Education in Derbeyshire before turning to research on the assessment of prior experiential learning. In 1980 he was a Senior Fellow for Policy Studies Institute. In 1986 he established the Learning from Experience Trust, of which he is the Director, as an education charity devoted to the development of work and the assessment of experiential learning. He has published many articles and books.

Chapter 11

Prior Learning Assessment in Québec Colleges

Robert Isabelle and Francine Landry

In 1982, a Study Commission on Adult Education recommended that the Québec government implement Prior Learning Assessment throughout its education system in order to facilitate access to the system for adults or their return to qualifying training.[1] Two years later, the government took three decisive steps. First, it published a policy statement on adult education which made an important priority of implementing Prior Learning Assessment in secondary schools, colleges and universities.[2] Then it added a section to the Regulation respecting the basis of college organization which stated that, starting on July 1, 1984, students could obtain credits for their non-academic learning. Finally, it agreed to subsidize a provincial structure of technical and financial support for colleges in order to implement and develop Prior Learning Assessment. That structure included a provincial implementation committee consisting of representatives of public colleges, private colleges, the Department of Higher Education and Science, as well as a Technical Assistance Service located at the Federation of Public Colleges.

Initial Goals and Priorities

From the outset, the colleges have intended to implement a system of Prior Learning Assessment which was credible (based on

---

[1] Study Commission on Adult Education. *Learning: a voluntary and responsible action. Statement of an overall adult education policy in a perspective of continuing education.* Montréal, 1982. 872 f.

[2] Québec (Province). Government. *Continuing Education Program Policy statement and plan of action.* Québec City, 1984. 75 f.

valid and reliable evaluations), comprehensive (utilizing different existing approaches), widely accessible and relatively inexpensive. They set themselves two main priorities: first, the training of people to be in charge of the matter in the colleges (administrators, counselors and evaluators), several workshops being given by experts from CAEL; second, use of the portfolio approach since that seemed to be the most all-inclusive, the most flexible and the best suited to individuals and to their prior learning of the experiential type.

Fund to Implement Prior Learning Assessment in Colleges

In January 1987, the Québec Department of Higher Education and Science and the Department of Employment and Immigration of Canada undertook to pay colleges subsidies of $1 million and $3 million dollars, respectively, over the next three years, in order to implement and develop Prior Learning Assessment. At the end of October 1987, the colleges created from these subsidies the Fund to Implement Prior Learning Assessment at the college level covering responsibilities which, until then, had been those of the previous provincial structure of technical and financial support for colleges; i.e., information, the sensitization and training of those involved, research, the elaboration of tools, assistance for the realization and evaluation of local projects, coordination of college projects, the financing of local projects and services, and liaison with Québec, Canadian and foreign organizations interested in Prior Learning Assessment.

Local Projects

Since 1985-1986, 44 college training establishments have undertaken Prior Learning Assessment projects, including 38 public colleges, four private colleges and two State establishments.[3] These projects are divided into three major categories.

---

[3] Québec has 44 public colleges (called CEGEPS; i.e., Colleges of General and Professional Education), 25 private colleges (the great majority of which have no Adult Education Service), and 10 State establishments (under a department other than that of Higher Education and Science).

The first category includes projects which tend to satisfy the prerequisites for implementing Prior Learning Assessment. This process involves forming a Local Committee, formulating operational guidelines (developing local policy and procedures), informing the staff, training counselors and evaluators and making adults aware of the possibility of, and their interest in obtaining credits for their non-academic prior learning.

The projects in the second category are those of colleges which have accomplished the above tasks and which are ready to implement, in a limited and experimental fashion, a service or system of Prior Learning Assessment. To date, the colleges concerned have opted for implementation based on the portfolio approach, on that of examinations, or on both approaches. At the same time, these colleges have undertaken a good number of operations affecting the screening interview for candidates, the administrative and pedagogical management of files, recruitment, training and payment for counselors and evaluators.

The projects in the third category are those involving the elaboration of a comprehensive program, the diversification of the "publics" served or the approaches used, the elaboration of out-of-class learning formulas, the grouping of colleges so as to offer better services at better costs, the elaboration of tools which can serve all college-education establishments (e.g., equivalency tables, standardized tests), the integration of Prior Learning Assessment with made-to-measure education, the elaboration of competency-based programs, or the elaboration of an integrated body of services including Prior Learning Assessment which are offered to adults, to companies, to industries and to various organizations.

The Programs and Disciplines Affected

Overall, about 40 professional programs have been affected by Prior Learning Assessment, as well as some disciplines in general education (French, mathematics, philosophy, psychology).[4] It is clearly the human techniques and the administrative techniques

---

[4] In Québec, colleges dispense vocational training programs (about 130) which last for three years and lead to the labor market, and general education programs (6) which last for two years and lead to university. All the programs include compulsory courses: French (language and literature), philosophy and physical education.

which have produced the greatest number of Prior Learning Assessment operations to date.

Developing the Tools

From the start, but especially in 1986-1987, much energy has been devoted to the elaboration of tools. This work involves, on one hand, screening-interview manuals, information manuals, administration manuals, portfolio manuals, evaluation report manuals, checklists to identify non-academic prior learning, policies and procedures, and, on the other hand, tools accurately measuring and evaluating non-academic learning in relation to the objectives of the programs and the courses given by the colleges.

For adults who have received non-establishment training in a formal setting (e.g., courses given by the armed forces, companies, industries, voluntary organizations or unions, etc.), some colleges have undertaken to elaborate equivalency manuals comparing this training and college-level courses. Drawing inspiration from the methodology developed by the American Council on Education, Collège Ahuntsic thus evaluated courses given by the armed forces involving three military trades and an association of medical electrophysiology, and allocated credits to people with official evidence of having succeeded in those courses.

However, the non-academic training of adults is usually of varied origin. So it seems necessary to identify the prior learning and to measure it using tools such as theoretical and practical examinations, performance tests, structured interviews, etc. Since the examinations used in class are usually inadequate to measure non-academic prior learning, the teachers must therefore often create new examinations, suited to the prior learning concerned. Before developing these examinations, it is almost always necessary to define the objectives of the courses and to determine the importance of these objectives when compared with others, all of which represents a great deal of work.

Some of these tools can be described as "house tools" since they are devised by a single teacher, for a particular context and using the means available, so that there is no guarantee that they can be used in another college even if they serve the purpose for which they were designed.

Other tools are conceived for use in several colleges; these are "national tools." That designation applies to the standardized

French tests being elaborated at Collège Marie-Victorin and the tests in education techniques for day-care developed by teachers in about 20 colleges and offered by those establishments.

Some tools straddle the above two types. They are developed locally by departments or teams of teachers and take into account several course plans. Some colleges have begun to exchange, lend or buy such tools. Another possibility being considered is to have the prior learning of candidates evaluated by the colleges which have the required evaluation tools available.

The situation is slightly different when a college decides on the portfolio as the favored or exclusive method. In fact, it is then up to the candidate himself or herself to demonstrate, first in writing, that the candidate can really master one or more courses. To date, most teachers who have evaluated non-academic prior learning from the portfolio have been faced with the rather inaccurate nature of their existing evaluation criteria. In this situation, the teachers have been obliged to revise their course objectives, to establish which are the main and which are secondary objectives, and finally to define more precise evaluation criteria which implement the objectives and which are relevant to the context of non-academic prior learning. Moreover, many teachers have considered it wise to submit candidates to a written examination or to an interview devised by the faculty in order to ensure that the candidates have completely attained the objectives of their courses.

Development of the Portfolio

Several colleges have given a credited 45-hour course on the development of the portfolio. Others have conceived the development of the portfolio as a group activity in a process of under 45 hours, or in an individualized process. Other colleges have asked candidates to prepare a written file in support of their applications without, however, describing that file as a "portfolio."

The development of a portfolio is not automatically produced with the submission of an application for evaluating non-academic prior learning. In order to understand this point, it must be borne in mind that the portfolio process also enables an adult to make contact with the college, to clarify his or her expectations, to specify a professional choice and to assess his or her prior learning at its correct value. In such a context, it is not surprising that some adults change their initial intentions and decide not to submit a portfolio to obtain credits.

Furthermore, some colleges have developed a shortened portfolio procedure. Thus, at the Collège du Vieux Montréal, about 15 hours of group work has enabled day-care workers to prepare their evaluation applications. At the École nationale d'aérotechnique, candidates prepare a file, course by course, with a minimum of supervision. Collège Montmorency has produced a video and accompanying document on the elaboration of the portfolio which should enable an adult to undertake this process independently.

Final Considerations

The implementation of Prior Learning Assessment in Québec colleges cannot be considered as a "fait accompli." The most advanced colleges are only at the stage of systematic experimentation in defining the appropriate operating methods and providing themselves with adequate working tools. Furthermore, by deliberate choice, the experiments being undertaken are limited to certain programs, and the number of applications processed is maintained at quite a low level. In addition, the basic problem of the stable financing of operating services or local Prior Learning Assessment systems will have to be satisfactorily resolved in the fairly near future. However, this implementation is definitely on the way to being realized. The evidence for this expectation can be seen in the number of colleges committed to the implementation process, the nature and scope of the work accomplished and the cooperation which has been developed between the colleges and the agencies of the Department of Manpower (i.e., the Vocational Training Commissions) which have begun to evaluate and sanction the professional skills of the workers. The colleges also maintain contact with both the secondary level, which is expanding and making official practices in Prior Learning Assessment which go back to 1977 more flexible, and the university level which, to date, has recognized non-academic learning almost only for purposes of admission and is starting to grant credits for such learning.

There is no doubt that Québec colleges would not have reached this point without CAEL. CAEL, first, partly inspired the recommendations of the Study Commission on Adult Education to implement Prior Learning Assessment throughout the Québec education system (1982). Then CAEL gave us a body of tried fundamental principles, as well as quality technical and human resources.

It is also possible that Québec colleges, in turn, may contribute to the implementation of Prior Learning Assessment beyond the borders of the province. The colleges of the other Canadian provinces are starting to show interest in what their Québec counterparts are doing and could well follow in their footsteps in the near future. The same applies to the Department of National Education in France which, in recent years, has sent and has hosted several working groups on Prior Learning Assessment.

But the main concern of Québec colleges remains to establish a quality system of Prior Learning Assessment and to ensure the best possible services for adults. Once that goal is achieved, they will be able to play a role in the international expansion of Prior Learning Assessment.

Robert Isabelle, a former college teacher and administrator, has also worked in the field of research and development. He is now Executive Director of the Fund for the Implementation of Prior Learning Assessment in Quebec Colleges.

Francine Landry is consultant for the Fund for the Implementation of Prior Learning Assessment in Quebec Colleges. Since 1983 she has shared in research and development of prior learning assessment in Quebec colleges and universities. She has authored many texts pertaining to prior learning assessment and distance learning.

Chapter 12
Learning Theory and the Benefits of Assessment

Barry Sheckley

Earlier chapters of this book have outlined ways the prior learning assessment (PLA) process benefits adult learners. This chapter will discuss how it can stimulate further learning by helping students understand limits of their knowledge. The following case study illustrates how prior learning assessment, by requiring a learner to assess critically some of the fundamental assumptions she uses in her job, makes her more open to new ideas.

In her first meeting with me, in my role as faculty reviewer, Thelma personified all the positive outcomes of the prior learning assessment process. Clearly she was proud of her accomplishments and confident that the assessment program would help her achieve new career goals. The validation she received through credit awards and the accompanying advanced placements played an important role in her decision to pursue a college degree.

She was requesting three credits for a Counseling 101 course on the basis of eight years of experience as a para-professional case worker with a community action agency. Before interviewing her about the learning outcomes documented in her portfolio, I asked that she send me a 10-15 minute audio tape of a simulated counseling session.

The tape revealed that Thelma equated counseling with advice giving. As her role-playing client attempted to describe a problem, Thelma continually interrupted to give quick fix solutions. Discussions with Thelma about the tape and the contents of her portfolio confirmed my belief. She felt that her role as a counselor was to tell people how to solve their problems on the basis of her own values, ideas and expertise. She had never considered counseling as a process of helping people solve their own problems. Reluctantly, I recommended that her credit request be denied.

Surprisingly, Thelma continued to visit me over the following semesters to chat about her progress and her career plans. On her final visit, just before graduation, she discussed ways the prior learning assessment process contributed to her learning. Thelma recollected how she entered the college full of self-doubt about her academic abilities. "After all, I was an 'old lady' with a full 16 years separating me from high school classrooms." Initially, the credit awards flooded her with self-esteem and confirmed that, indeed, she was not "stupid." The advanced placements helped remove fears that completing the college degree would take a lifetime.

Thelma also told me how the assessment process had opened her eyes to what she didn't know. At first she didn't see evaluations like mine as useful. The recommendations to deny her credit only infuriated her and made her want to leave the college. As she progressed in her coursework the value of the process became more evident. Her academic journey confirmed the prior learning assessment lesson that learning involved more than just acquiring new bits of information. Many times she had to "unlearn" her previous assumptions before she could learn new ideas. Unexpectedly, this insight became a more valuable outcome of the portfolio assessment process for her than the credits she earned.

With this discussion, Thelma gave me a new perspective on the value of prior learning assessment and made me wonder whether or how it could be explained on the basis of theories of adult learning.

Prior Learning Assessment and Adult Learning Theory

The American psychologist William James, once commented: "A great many people think they are thinking when they are merely rearranging their predjudices." Similarly, as was evident in the first stages of Thelma's learning, many adults believe they are learning when they simply rearrange their ideas or modify their customary ways of acting. They often think of learning in terms of successful experiences and not in terms of the learning acquired from the experiences. While Thelma had eight years of counseling experiences, she did not have an equivalent eight years of learning from those experiences.

Experience alone does not generate new learning; neither does the college classroom. Learning requires the adult to relate new situations to previous ones and new information to ingrained ways of thinking. Not surprisingly, adults frequently resist this way of learning.

Psychological research demonstrates that we will not alter our perceptions until we are frustrated in our attempts to apply them successfully (Postman and Weingartner, 1968). Adult learners enter college programs with records of successful accomplishments in the world. They are reluctant to abandon their life-tested strategies for textbook solutions. Stephen Brookfield (1987), however, emphasizes that such reflection is essential for adult development. In a recent book he insightfully discusses how "Thinking critically—reflecting on the assumptions underlying our and others' ideas and actions, and contemplating alternative ways of thinking and living—is one of the important ways in which we become adults." Prior learning assessment is an excellent way for adults to begin a critical assessment of the assumptions they use in their daily lives.

The information processing model of learning (Ivey, 1986) illustrates why the prior learning assessment process is an effective learning tool. Simply stated, the model shows that prior learning assessment stimulates the two channels which comprise adult learning.

Figure 1
Information Processing Model of Learning

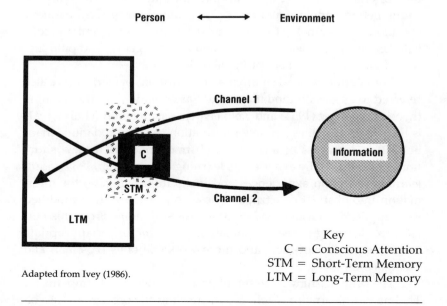

Adapted from Ivey (1986).

Key
C = Conscious Attention
STM = Short-Term Memory
LTM = Long-Term Memory

Figure 1 illustrates how consciousness and memory interact to use information. Conscious attention involves the brief (less than 1 second) focus on a particular stimulus in the environment. Conscious impressions can be maintained for up to 10 seconds in short term memory. Also referred to as "telephone memory" (since we use it to retain 7 numbers for the period between reading them in the directory and dialing the phone), short term memory can hold up to 100 items in a buffer space until they are filtered into long term memory. The storehouse of our permanent knowledge, long term memory, is a highly selective information processor.

The usual approach to promoting college learning uses learning channel #1 (Figure 1). The teacher provides compelling lectures, exciting slide shows, or dynamic audio tapes to capture students' conscious attention. The student acquires or "learns" the information through repetition and written exercises which pass it through short term into long term memory.

Adults tend to resist the channel #1 (information acquisition) model of learning by rejecting or selectively filtering new information. They find learning channel #2 much more appealing (Figure 1). When learners like Thelma enter college programs they like to begin the learning process by using information already stored in their long term memory. Since 30 to 40 years can be invested in long term memory banks, adults understandably prefer to tap these vaults before adding new items. Consequently long term memory can monitor channel #1 circuits in the manner of a cantankerous gate keeper urging learners like Thelma to doggedly hold onto life-honed ideas instead of adopting new viewpoints.

The channel #1 and channel #2 descriptions of learning are also referred to as "accommodation" and "assimilation" in the learning theories of Piaget (1954) and Kolb (1984). Assimilation (channel #1) is the process of taking in new information. Accommodation (channel #2) is a process of testing out abstract concepts in new situations. As outlined by experiential learning theory (Kolb, 1984), adult learners reflect on experiences and integrate (assimilate) the information into abstract constructs. These concepts are then modified with application (accommodation) to new situations. From this perspective, learning is seen as the ability to relinquish inappropriate ideas and to develop new and more workable ones (Postman and Weingartner, 1968).

The prior learning assessment process provided the impetus for Thelma to unlearn approaches to counseling she brought to the college and then relearn different skills by using a channel to describe her working theories of counseling. Subsequent feedback helped her understand limitations in her counseling skills and make her more receptive to traditional channel #1 presentations. As Thelma herself admitted, the prior learning assessment feedback process was an important first step in her development of more complex counseling skills.

Whenever I think of the ways prior learning assessment contributes to the adult learning process, I remember that last meeting I had with Thelma. As she turned to leave my office that graduation day, she gave me another audio tape which captured her development as a counselor. It was a gift, she said, for the worlds of new learning which opened each time she stopped to assess the assumptions which guided her behavior. This tape was a living testimony to the power of prior learning assessment as a learning event.

References

Brookfield, Stephen D. *Developing Critical Thinkers*. San Francisco: Jossey Bass, 1987.

Ivey, A. *Developmental Therapy*. San Francisco: Jossey Bass, 1986.

Kolb, David *Experiential Learning*. Englewood Cliffs: Prentice Hall, 1984.

Piaget, Jean *The Construction of Reality in the Child*. New York: Basic Books, 1954.

Postman, N. and Weingartner, C. *Teaching as a Subversive Activity*. New York: Delacorte Press, 1968.

Barry Sheckley is Assistant Professor for the Adult and Vocational Program, in the School of Education, at the University of Connecticut. He was the Regional Manager for CAEL Northeast and is now Staff Research Associate for CAEL.